Introducing RavenDB

The Database for Modern Data Persistence

Dejan Miličić

Apress®

Introducing RavenDB: The Database for Modern Data Persistence

Dejan Miličić
Novi Sad, Serbia

ISBN-13 (pbk): 978-1-4842-8918-1   ISBN-13 (electronic): 978-1-4842-8919-8
https://doi.org/10.1007/978-1-4842-8919-8

Managing Director, Apress Media LLC: Welmoed Spahr
Acquisitions Editor: Jonathan Gennick
Development Editor: Laura Berendson
Coordinating Editor: Jill Balzano

Cover Photo by WrongTog on Unsplash

Distributed to the book trade worldwide by Springer Science+Business Media LLC, 1 New York Plaza, Suite 4600, New York, NY 10004. Phone 1-800-SPRINGER, fax (201) 348-4505, e-mail orders-ny@springer-sbm.com, or visit www.springeronline.com. Apress Media, LLC is a California LLC and the sole member (owner) is Springer Science + Business Media Finance Inc (SSBM Finance Inc). SSBM Finance Inc is a **Delaware** corporation.

For information on translations, please e-mail booktranslations@springernature.com; for reprint, paperback, or audio rights, please e-mail bookpermissions@springernature.com.

Apress titles may be purchased in bulk for academic, corporate, or promotional use. eBook versions and licenses are also available for most titles. For more information, reference our Print and eBook Bulk Sales web page at http://www.apress.com/bulk-sales.

Any source code or other supplementary material referenced by the author in this book is available to readers on GitHub. For more detailed information, please visit http://www.apress.com/source-code.

Printed on acid-free paper

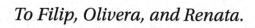

To Filip, Olivera, and Renata.

Table of Contents

About the Author

 **Dejan Miličić** is a consultant with more than 20 years' experience as a professional software developer. His experience includes designing, writing, and maintaining applications, focusing on software architecture and backend development. He advocates domain-driven design, behavior-driven development, functional programming, and API-first development.

Miličić's passion for RavenDB goes back to 2015, when he started using this NoSQL database for small hobby projects and quickly realized it is applicable to a wide range of applications. He specializes in RavenDB because it is well suited for fast prototyping and development of everything from line-of-business applications to large enterprise distributed systems.

About the Technical Reviewer

 **Chris Woodruff** (or Woody as he is commonly known) has a degree in computer science from Michigan State University's College of Engineering. Woody has been developing and architecting software solutions for over 20 years and has worked on many platforms and tools. He is a community leader, helping such events as GRDevNight, GRDevDay, West Michigan Day of .NET, and Beer City Code. He was also instrumental in bringing the popular Give Camp event to Western Michigan, where technology professionals lend their time and development expertise to assist local nonprofits. As a speaker and podcaster, Woody has discussed various topics, including database design and open source. He has been a Microsoft MVP in Visual C#, Data Platform, and SQL and was recognized in 2010 as one of the top 20 MVPs worldwide. Woody is an Engineering Team Leader for Rocket Homes and leads a team building out a new Enterprise Service Bus for the company.

Acknowledgments

I want to express my gratitude to Jonathan Gennick and Jill Balzano from Apress for approaching me with the idea of writing this book and supporting me patiently along the way, which was not always smooth.

My most profound appreciation goes to Oren Eini, Paweł Pekról, and Arkadiusz Paliński.

Through numerous discussions, Marcin Lewandowski, Danielle Greenberg, Grzegorz Lachowski, and Igal Merhavia answered all my questions and helped me clarify concepts and ideas.

Discussions with Đorđe Đukić, Aleksandar Sabo, Shahar Erez, and Federico Lois have been illuminating.

Christopher Balnave, Igor Ivanović, and David Ben Horin read early drafts; their remarks were helpful.

This book wouldn't have been possible without support from my family: my wife Renata, my daughter Olivera, and my son Filip, who have supported and encouraged me.

Introduction

When was the last time you paid attention to the windows in your home? Probably when they were dirty and needed cleaning, or if one of them got broken and needed replacement. But, if everything is okay with them, you will not pay attention.

A good database is like a window. It "just works." It is fast and reliable without needing you to be a database expert. In the ideal scenario, you will not pay attention to it - you will concentrate on doing your business, and a database is there to support you.

For the past 40+ years, we have been using relational databases. It would be natural to think that we mastered them to the extent that an average developer can build applications that scale as the organization grows, supporting ever-increasing traffic volume and data volume. Additionally, with the emergence of web applications in the 1990s, we have a potentially unbounded audience, and terabytes are new gigabytes.

Even if you have years of experience with relational databases, you already know what awaits you at the very start of the project: queries that join multiple tables (sometimes up to seven or eight of them), caching layer to compensate for slow queries, numerous performance problems as the amount of data in the database grows over time, the additional layer of data persistence modeling.

It is not uncommon even for application developers with 20+ years of experience to run into 20% of requests which are permanently slow because of a relational database. And then, they live the Pareto principle - spending 80% of maintenance time nurturing that 20% of code not working fast enough. Over time, this grows into insecurity and chronic imposter syndrome.

If only you were an expert, it would be much easier! But you are not an expert. You do not have months to spend digging deep into the internals of the database. You do not want to work on optimizing the database. You want to work on developing your application.

RavenDB is a database created with this goal – to empower you to produce outstanding results without needing to become an expert in databases. Expert knowledge is embedded, so the database will assist you, advise you, and safeguard you as you develop your application. Most common antipatterns (like full table scans) are actively prevented.

I encountered RavenDB a decade ago and fell in love with it over the years. I discovered that RavenDB is suitable for small projects, fast prototyping, and scaling to enterprise-grade Domain-Driven Design projects.

This book is a gentle introduction to NoSQL concepts. Starting from zero, you will learn the basics of RavenDB, the NoSQL document database, its query language, and the indexing engine. You will also discover how RavenDB reacts to your operational behavior, protecting and guiding you. After completing this book, you will be capable of installing RavenDB and using it for efficiently storing and querying data.

To follow the content of this book, you do not need anything but modern web browsers and elementary knowledge of JavaScript. You will grasp NoSQL principles (like map/reduce) and comprehend RavenDB mechanisms. After you finish it, you can easily apply this knowledge to building applications in any modern programming language.

So, let's dive into the fantastic world of RavenDB together!

CHAPTER 1

Getting Started with RavenDB

In the narrow sense of the word, a *database* is a collection of information. In a broader meaning of that term, *database management system (DBMS)* is what we usually think about when we talk about "database" - a system providing means for manipulating databases to define, store, manage, and retrieve data.

Although many developers still consider relational database to be the "golden standard," they are just one phase in the history of data persistence solutions. This chapter will go over a brief historical overview of DBMS and their origins, development, and produced solutions. As you will see, relational databases emerged as a solution to one set of problems. In the same way, engineers created NoSQL databases to solve the next-generation set of challenges.

Finally, we will introduce RavenDB as a second-generation NoSQL database and look at its origins, history, and some of the features that make RavenDB an excellent choice both for small projects and large enterprise systems.

A Brief History of Databases

Since the first days of computing, machines have produced computation results and persisted them. Over time, different solutions for storing data emerged. Still, all these systems were tightly coupled to hardware and operating system to maximize the speed at the expense of flexibility and standardization. As hardware continued to evolve, this compromise was increasingly unnecessary, and many general-purpose DBMS emerged. One of the first such systems, Integrated Data Store (IDS), was developed by Charles Bachman in the early 1960s, using the Navigational Database Model.

© Dejan Miličić 2022
D. Miličić, *Introducing RavenDB*, https://doi.org/10.1007/978-1-4842-8919-8_1

In June of 1970, Edgar F. Codd published the seminal paper "A Relational Model of Data for Large Shared Data Banks," where he introduced the Relational Database Management System (RDBMS). The importance of his groundbreaking idea lies in the concept of describing data only with its natural structure, avoiding the need to superimpose any additional structures for low-level machine representation. This high level of data representation provides a basis for high-level data language, giving such programs independence from low-level details of machine representation and RDBMS internal data organization.

Unlike the navigational approach that required programs to loop to collect records, Codd's solution provided set-oriented declarative language. This approach led to the birth of Structured Query Language - SQL - in 1974. Following this standardization, Oracle released the first commercial implementation of SQL in 1979.

A landmark year for the relational model was 1980 when IBM released their product for mainframes, and smaller vendors began selling second-generation relational systems with great commercial success. During the 1980s, RDBMSes finally came of age and established themselves as the first choice for large datasets typically present in government agencies and financial institutions. Furthermore, relational persistence became a default pick by developers around the world.

Problems with Relational DBMS

However, as is the case with any technology, there is no such thing as a "silver bullet." Various problems are calling for different solutions. Non-relational databases, which existed before relational databases became dominant persistence solutions, continued to live. Since the late 1960s, hierarchical, graph, and object-oriented databases have been around. The reason for this is that RDBMS has several challenges:

- Relational databases work best with structured data stored in well-organized tables. For unstructured data, tables with fixed predefined schema are not the best choice.

- Users can scale a relational database by running it on more powerful (and expensive) servers. This approach is "scaling up" and is feasible up to a certain point. After that, a database must be distributed across multiple servers – "scaling out." Relational databases are inherently single-server databases, and distributed solutions are not elegant and seamless.

- Relational databases do not natively support data partitioning and distributed setup. ACID transactions that are the basis of RDBMS are fundamentally clashing with distributed computing.

Impedance Mismatch

When developing computer software, developers are modeling data structures that represent an abstraction of the real-life domain. These models (which are part of objects in object-oriented languages) are nonlinear and almost always contain complex constructs like collections of primitive values or nested objects containing other primitive values. On the other hand, many popular relational databases cannot store anything beyond scalar values (like numbers and strings). As a result, relational databases cannot directly store and manipulate your objects and data structures. This incompatibility is a very well-known phenomenon and has been named *impedance mismatch*.

Before you can store your objects into a relational database, you need to transform them into a set of structures matching your RDBMS schema. And the other way around - data in tables and rows need to be manipulated and reshaped to populate objects. So, storing things into a relational database and fetching them again require a process of two-way translation.

This translation occurs between two models - your (usually object-oriented) domain model and tabular model intended for saving into your database.

Hence, developers need to create an additional data model and provide a bidirectional translation service. Also, every time they make corrections or changes to their primary domain model, they need to update this translation logic. Modeling twice and maintaining translation service are a nontrivial task that will make changes harder, and that will make you move slower in the face of ever-coming change requests from your customers.

Object-Relational Mappers

Object-relational mapper (ORM) is a tool that can automate this tedious task of translating the data from its relational representation into the object model used by the application. However, as every developer using many of numerous ORMS like Hibernate or Entity Framework knows, there are many downsides to these libraries:

- ORM is abstracting away RDBMS details, so over time developer inevitably starts thinking about the database as a collection of data in memory.

- Generated SQL statements are inferior to handwritten SQL.

- There is an inevitable overhead of ORM.

- Initial configuration of ORM can be complicated.

In his 2006 blog post "The Vietnam of Computer Science," Ted Neward wrote

> *Object/Relational Mapping is the Vietnam of Computer Science. It represents a quagmire which starts well, gets more complicated as time passes, and before long entraps its users in a commitment that has no clear demarcation point, no clear win conditions, and no clear exit strategy*

Indeed, over time as your application grows and expands, ORM usage will lead to the accumulation of antipatterns.

Select N+1 is just one of those antipatterns. Your code will first fetch N entities from the database, then iterate over this collection, making additional calls for every object to bring other referenced things. A typical example would be a web page where you are rendering the list of articles. Each of these articles has comments, and you need to make an additional call to the database to fetch the latest comment to show along with each piece. Furthermore, you would like to display the location of the comment author. As you can see, there is a cascading set of parent-child relations, and in every step, you are accessing the next level, descending hierarchy, and making more and more calls.

Normalization

Normalization is a modeling technique that is an essential part of Codd's model of relational databases. In the early 1970s, storage was expensive, and eliminating data redundancy was a critical design factor for a database system designer.

Codd defined first (1NF), second (2NF), and third (*3NF*) *normal forms* as a theoretical basis for best practices of data modeling. With the application of 3NF principles, you will eliminate redundancy by breaking records into their most atomic form, store those pieces in separate tables, and then relate them via *Foreign Keys* (FK).

FK is nothing more than a pointer. For example, when storing customers in the *Customers* table, you would separate their address and keep it in the *Address* table. Then, you would create FK to connect these two tables to establish a relationship between the row in the Customers table and the row in Address table containing the customer's address.

After developing a concept of normalization to eliminate data redundancy, Codd constructed a mathematical theory of normalization and provided theoretical guarantees about 3NF providing data consistency and preventing anomalies when inserting, updating, and deleting rows.

Today, storage is cheap. Not only that, your server's RAM will most likely have dozens of gigabytes at your disposal, usually in the range of your database size. Good DBMS will detect this and optimize it by loading large parts of your database to working memory. So, over time, redundancy faded away as a motivation for normalization, and today you will hear relational database proponents speaking about 3NF only in the context of database consistency.

However, normalization leads to several problems, and two of them are major ones.

The first challenge is related to *projections*. Every time you need to display a web page that contains complex data, you will have to create a projection – a combination of rows from different tables. For example, to show an invoice, you will have to combine data from several tables, including Invoices, Customers, Addresses, Products, and Employees. Joining five tables is not a demanding operation. Still, once you load your database with tens of thousands of invoices and when you start creating aggregations that are answering questions like "what are the top 5 countries where we export to," you will notice performance degradation of your RDBMS. Hence, projections in relational databases are putting a load on the developer and on the database itself.

A second major problem of normalization is *temporal snapshots*. As we already mentioned, RDBMS are priding themselves with a solid theoretical background that guarantees that data will not be corrupted. However, a straightforward example will show you how normalization is fragile in the light of changes that your data undergo over time. Returning to the story of invoices modeled with a normalized approach, we can see that Invoices are residing in one table, pointing to the Companies table. Further,

Companies are related to the Countries table that contains a list of all countries. This way, Invoices are related to Countries via Companies. Now, imagine that Company relocates from London to Berlin – you will go into the Companies table and change FK related to the Countries table to point to the row containing Germany.

This simple change should not have dramatic consequences. However, due to normalized modeling, the modification you just performed has a rippling effect. Although you did not touch Invoices in this process, they are affected since they are related to the Company that changed address. As a result, next time you repeat that aggregation, "what are the top 5 countries where we export to," you may discover that the United Kingdom is not there anymore. In other words – by making a simple change to the address of one Company, you introduced data corruption on a historical level.

Normalization is incapable of modeling temporal dependencies of this kind. To store a snapshot of your invoice, you will have to apply the denormalization process. Finally, we can conclude that, instead of bringing promised consistency and validity of your data, normalization will corrupt your historical data.

Modern Web Applications

In the 1970s and 1980s, data arriving at your application was predictable and highly structured. With the emergence of the Internet and the globalization of your user base, things started developing more rapidly. Today, modern Internet applications serve a wide variety of users, offering many services and evolving rapidly. Having hundreds of concurrent users of your application is nothing strange.

Twenty or 30 years ago, you would experience this only with applications deployed to large enterprises. Thirty years ago, you would receive a Requirements Specification document with a precisely defined schema of the data you need to store in the relational database. Then you would apply waterfall methodology, spend months implementing it, and finally release it. Today, you are working in 2-week sprints, with change requests coming merely days after delivering working functionality.

Relational databases, in their nature, were optimized for writing data. Reading data was a secondary priority. Modern web applications will commonly store data once and then request it dozens or hundreds of times before making another write. Data that was disassembled into atomic units and stored over dozens of tables during the writing process now needs to be reassembled again to produce a model for rendering information on a web page. And this is not happening just once. Thousands of visitors to your web application will trigger many such calls.

Rendering modern web pages will generate many requests to the database. These same users who are requesting pages will also interact with your application and generate new data that will be stored. Think about a small mom-and-pop shop two decades ago – they are running one POS, with a number of transactions limited by the physical factors – customers standing in line, one customer at a time. Small shop managed to survive and expand, and it is now online. There are no more limitations of physical nature; they are now in a virtual world where 50 customers can purchase within 3 minutes.

The relational database model was conceived at different times – fewer read requests, more occasional users, highly structured data, and slow pace of changes to your application. You could say that the present situation is the opposite.

NoSQL

Problems we just described grew only more painful over time. As the pace of change requests sped up, as the number of users and amount of data grew exponentially, it was clear that we needed some alternatives. It was evident that RDBMS were not the most suitable solution in all cases and that some systems required different approaches for storing and querying data.

This section will look into the evolution that emerged in the 1990s and 2000s and lead to creating the NoSQL movement. We will examine the origins of *NoSQL* as a term, the advantages and challenges of such a database, and, finally, the broader impact of this movement on the whole industry.

Origins of "NoSQL" Name

NoSQL databases are a further evolution of databases. You could say that databases you can characterize as "non-relational" existed before the invention of RDBMS. However, the NoSQL movement is not returning to these historical solutions; they represent further advancement in data persistence solutions.

Ironically, the NoSQL acronym was first used as a name of Relational Database Management System built by Carlo Strozzi in 1998. NoSQL name was inspired by the fact that this system was not a database but rather a shell-level tool, with data in regular UNIX ASCII files that various UNIX utilities and editors could manipulate. Hence, the intentional lack of support for SQL as a query language was an inspiration for the name.

Johan Oskarsson was the first to use "NoSQL" that we recognize today. He was seeking a name for a meetup he organized in San Francisco in June 2009. This meetup showcased a number of non-relational distributed databases. In subsequent months and years, the term "NoSQL" was adopted, but it was never standardized or defined precisely, so we can only discuss some general characteristics exposed by the databases belonging to this broad category.

Why NoSQL?

As we will see, NoSQL represents a broad category of heterogeneous approaches to solving problems that emerged in the late 2000s. During that period

- Web applications emerged, and data started arriving in all forms and shapes - structured, semi-structured, unstructured, and polymorphic. Defining comprehensive schema upfront became almost impossible, or in the best case, such attempts resulted in solutions that were cumbersome to work with and hard for maintenance over the long run.

- The cost of storage dramatically decreased. Data duplication on the database level was no longer a determining factor for creating complex and complicated data models. Rather than disk storage, developers and their valuable time became the primary cost factor of software development. Optimizing for productivity instead of storage space was the main driving factor.

- Cloud computing rose in popularity in the late 2000s and became a legitimate choice for hosting applications and data. As developers started distributing data across multiple servers, they needed a way to scale out instead of scale-up, make their applications resilient, and geo-distribute data in the proximity of their users.

- Agile Manifesto was gaining traction, and rapidly changing requirements were looked upon not as a disturbing factor but as a fact of the developer's life that needs to be accepted, embraced, and incorporated into the development cycle. Software engineers worldwide started recognizing a need to change their code quickly, and reshaping of persisted data was an integral part of that effort. NoSQL databases found their place in this puzzle as a flexible solution that could provide less painful pivot and remodeling on the fly.

Characteristics

The term *NoSQL* today describes a variety of database technologies that emerged to cater demands of modern applications. They all share some common traits:

- The first and most obvious point is the negation in the name - NoSQL databases are not using SQL, in the sense of being *non-relational.*

- NoSQL databases emerged from the open source community. Although today you can find NoSQL solutions coming from closed-source producers like IBM, Oracle, and Amazon, in general, NoSQL databases are primarily open source projects.

- Most NoSQL databases are supporting cluster setup, which has a significant impact on their approach to consistency and data modeling.

- NoSQL databases do not have a mandatory schema, so fields in records can be added and removed without a need to define changes in the structures first.

- They are based on the needs of modern web applications, where a massive number of concurrent users can store a humongous amount of data that can have different shapes and form.

These are broad characteristics, and due to the heterogeneous nature of these databases, there is a low chance we will ever have a definitive coherent definition.

Additional Advantages

Besides solving problems we already described, NoSQL databases are also offering some additional advantages:

- *Scaling out* - buying more powerful servers as database load increases – known as *scaling up* - has been a standard approach with relational databases over the years. However, as transaction rates and availability requirements increase, NoSQL databases offer a different solution. *Scaling out* is the approach of distributing databases across multiple servers or virtualized environments. Most RDBMS requests specialized or expensive hardware to scale up, while NoSQL databases can scale out cheap commodity hardware.

- *Economics* – traditionally, RDBMS has been relying on expensive proprietary servers and storage systems. Most NoSQL databases are open source licensed. Combined with the already mentioned ability to run on cheap commodity servers, even toy machines like Raspberry Pi, the total cost of ownership and cost per gigabyte or transactions per second are much lower with NoSQL DBMS.

- *Big data* - over the last decade, modern applications increased the volume of persisted data immensely. RDBMS capacity has been growing to match this demand, but constraints of specific relational systems became the limiting factor for enterprises. Presently, the capacity of "big data" NoSQL solutions like Hadoop surpasses the capabilities of the most significant RDBMS systems.

- *Administration* - NoSQL databases are, in most cases, designed from the ground up with clear intention to require less attention and administration compared to relational ones. Simpler data models, automatic maintenance, data distribution, and internal reconfiguration based on the environmental factors eliminate the need for a dedicated full-time DBA (Database Administrator). Despite numerous improvements in the manageability of relational systems, organizations using RDBMS still need the expertise of specialized personnel who will install, design, and maintain RDBMS. Of course, NoSQL databases are still requesting a certain level of knowledge from their users. Still, they eliminate mandatory expertise for someone to be able to run an efficient database-powered system.

Challenges

No technology is a silver bullet, and the adoption of any new technological paradigm has other aspects. Here are some challenges related to the adoption of NoSQL databases:

- *Maturity* - RDBMS has been around for over four decades now. They are well developed, mature, and stable, reassuring for most of the users. The mentality of the expression "nobody ever got fired for buying IBM" from the 1970s lives up to this day - RDBMS is perceived as a "safe choice," and NoSQL is looked upon as gambling with new "cool" technology. From the perspective of many companies, NoSQL is a unique, young technology, cutting edge that may be exciting for developers, but a big unknown in production.

- *Support* - in case of a system failure, competent and timely support is vital for every organization's business continuity plan. All RDBMS vendors go to great lengths to provide such support. On the other hand, many NoSQL products are open source and lack business entities that offer support options. When they exist, these companies are small startups without global presence, support resources, or credibility of an IBM, Oracle, or Microsoft.

- *Analytics and business intelligence* - data presents a valuable resource for every Company. They are analyzing data, mining, and making conclusions that improve their decision-making processes, efficiency, and, as a result, profitability in the market. Business intelligence (BI) is a strategic area for most companies. Over the years, the primary functionality of RDBMS has been augmented by a rich ecosystem of products offering additional BI services for analysis of the data. It is only recently that NoSQL DBMS started to catch up, offering similar solutions.

Outcome

The emergence of NoSQL databases did not eliminate the need for relational databases. Instead, it helped us reach a nondogmatic and balanced standpoint that there are other legitimate and reliable choices for data persistence.

This mental liberation started in 2006 when Neal Ford coined the term *Polyglot Programming*. This idea promotes implementing applications in multiple languages, understanding that specific problems could be solved in more straightforward and more convenient ways via different languages. Simply said - different programming languages are more suitable than others in solving particular problems.

Polyglot persistence is a concept that follows the same philosophy. Different situations and circumstances may call for other ways to model and store persisted data. Also, very often, one business domain can be split into multiple subdomains. Various data models might be the best representation of different subdomains. Polyglot persistence philosophy acknowledges this and eliminates compromising on data models to squeeze them all inside just one database.

So, instead of selecting a relational database for your next project as a default solution without too much thinking, you need to consider the nature of the data, business scenarios, and how you plan to manipulate data and then consider the best match among various technologies for persisting data. Consequently, organizations are moving from the concept of the database as an integration point and coming toward application databases, ending up with a mix of technologies that are serving different needs by different applications.

This mental liberation further flourished with the emergence of domain-driven design and microservices, where one solution consists of several databases, which can be a mix of persistence technologies. That way, databases are encapsulating data within applications, and services are performing integration.

NoSQL Database Types

As we already mentioned, various non-relational databases are using different approaches to solving needs for storing and querying data. There are four main types of NoSQL databases, with each type solving a problem that relational databases can't address adequately.

Key-Value Stores (KVS)

Prominent examples: Redis, Memcached, and CosmosDB

In some scenarios, using a full-blown database with powerful indexing and data retrieval would be overkill. You are looking for a quick and easy way to take an arbitrary piece of information, label it with a key, and store it in the database. Later, when you present a key, the database will deliver you associated value.

Key-value stores are databases, but highly specialized ones, built with just one purpose and deliberately constrained in design and functionality. Some are intentionally minimal, like Memcached, which is not even storing data on a disk. Others, like CosmosDB, added more features over time but are still based around the key-value paradigm.

Overall, key-value stores are intended for elementary tasks like caching or sharing common data between application services. Many relational databases can be used as a key-value store, but they would consume lots of resources and be more inefficient than specialized solutions. You would be overprovisioning resources and power in the same way if you would use an 18-wheeler for grocery shopping.

Document Stores (DS)

Prominent examples: MongoDB, RavenDB, Couchbase, and DocumentDB

Expanding on the capabilities provided by key-value stores, document stores can not only persist and retrieve information but also comprehend its structure. In the terminology of DS, documents are semi-structured data that are representing your business objects. You can index, manage, and manipulate documents based on their internal structure.

DS is aware of your documents' internal structure, so you can query your business partners by the address city, while KVS would provide just a way to store and retrieve them.

Relational databases force you to artificially split your objects into multiple sub-entities, which are then stored in tables and rows. DS can accept your documents in their natural form, index them, and provide you with means of creating projections producing the same results as JOINs in RDBMS but much more efficiently.

Before storing, your objects will be serialized to some standard format or encoding. Common encodings include JSON, XML, YAML, as well as a binary format like BSON.

Graph Databases (GD)

Prominent examples: Neo4j, OrientDB, TigerGraph, and ArangoDB

A graph is a mathematical structure representing a set of objects in which pairs of objects are related. Graph databases are implementing this concept, treating relationships between entities equally important as entities themself. Hence, GD is suitable for all those business domains where relationships are the crux of your model.

Graph databases are highly specialized NoSQL databases. You could say that they are building on the basis established by relational databases, bringing connections and relations between them to the status of full citizenship in the world of databases. Hence, besides data, GD contains metadata, or "data about data," and this metadata often matters more than the data itself.

With GD, independently of the total size of your dataset, you can efficiently explore highly connected data, perform searches based on patterns, and isolate your interactions with the data to just a tiny subset.

Wide-Column Stores (WCS)

Prominent examples: Bigtable, DynamoDB, Cassandra, ScyllaDB, and HBase

This category is also known under the name *extensible record stores*. Similar to relational databases, WCS is using tables, rows, and columns. However, columns are not fixed, and records can have billions of columns if needed. From the perspective of the key-value store, you could say that WCS is a two-dimensional KVS.

Multi-Model Databases

Multi-model databases are not the fifth category of NoSQL databases, but an emerging trend first mentioned in 2012 by Luca Garulli. Starting from Polyglot persistence, he envisioned a second generation of NoSQL databases, where one product supports different data models. This approach would combine the NoSQL ideal of selecting the most appropriate persistence for each subdomain of your application without having several different databases. Hence, you would not compromise in modeling and would end up with just one database to learn and manage.

Database choice is fraught with difficulty and risk since this choice is committed to a particular model upfront. Considering the fast pace of changes modern applications must support, this choice can be easily invalidated by unpredictable future changes.

Going with a multi-model database means that database choice can be less risky. Your database will be able to support you in various circumstances as your data model evolves under the stream of change requests you receive from your customers over time.

RavenDB

In this section, we will introduce RavenDB, a second-generation NoSQL database. You will learn about its history, why RavenDB is a good choice of data persistence for your applications, as well as how to start working with RavenDB in no time.

History

RavenDB was created by Oren Eini, a developer from Israel. In the late 2000s, he was an active contributor on the NHibernate project, .Net port of famous Hibernate ORM, one of the most popular mappers used by developers worldwide. Besides being involved in the open source community, Oren worked as a consultant for companies using relational databases. Being a prolific blogger under the pseudonym Ayende Rahien at `https://ayende.com`, he recorded various experiences with companies he was helping. It felt like one long Groundhog Day – they all had problems with applications, and canonical RDBMS caused all these problems most of us experienced – lack of indexes, Select N+1, projections that *JOIN*ed seven or eight tables… Could it be that so many developers were using relational databases in the wrong way? Or is there something inherently problematic with them? Do you need to be an expert in databases to develop your application swiftly and produce a solution that will be long-lasting and reliable?

It is not uncommon for software developers to observe problems over time, think about them, and become passionate about solving them. You could say that RavenDB was born equal parts from frustration with the present state of database landscape and passion for creating an elegant solution to practical problems.

In May 2010, Oren released version 1.0 of RavenDB. In October, the first commercial installation was secured, and after that, RavenDB started gaining popularity – up to the point when 1 million developers' downloads were reached in September 2015.

Today, RavenDB is a mature and reliable database, battle-proven from installations on small machines like Raspberry Pi up to clusters consisting of over a million nodes. Let's look at some reasons that helped RavenDB become such a versatile database.

Advantages of RavenDB

Along with all the advantages RavenDB has as a Document NoSQL database, which we discussed in previous sections, some specifics make it stand out.

Extreme Performance

RavenDB is highly optimized. Even on toy machines like Raspberry Pi 400, you will be able to serve over 2.000 concurrent read requests per second. Commodity hardware will bring you to 150.000 writes/s and 1.000.000 reads/s, and all of that with low latency. Furthermore, your queries will continuously operate over precomputed indexes so that you will get your results blazingly fast.

Fully Transactional

Since the very beginning, RavenDB is offering fully transactional ACID guarantees. Multi-document and multicollection transactions are supported as well, along with cluster-wide transactions. We will cover ACID in later chapters, but now, let's say – ACID is a bare minimum that any database should guarantee. It will ensure that your data is not lost and that your database maintains its consistency despite all challenges.

Auto Tuning

RavenDB is a grown-up database that knows how to take care of itself. If you try to execute a query without an index that will support it, RavenDB will create an index for you. If one node of your cluster gets slower for some reason, traffic will be redirected to the fastest node dynamically. Your cluster is on constant and ongoing self-monitoring mode. It will track vital parameters like CPU usage or memory utilization and act upon them. Overall, RavenDB is observing its environment and reacting intelligently.

Safe by Default

Being safe by default has many aspects, and RavenDB prides itself on state-of-the-art technical solutions and a set of defaults that will enable you to get up and to run in a matter of minutes. It is not only what you have to do but also a list of things you are not forced to do to produce safe applications. Here is the subset of these features:

- *Encryption* - default encryption in transit and optional encryption at rest mean that your data will never be exposed in plain text form to anyone who might listen to the traffic between your application and RavenDB.

- *Authentication* – X.509 digital certificates are used for access control as well as a basis for HTTPS access to the RavenDB cluster.

- *Limiting the number of database calls per session* – too many requests per single database session is dangerous. If developers are not careful, antipatterns like Select N+1 can result in dozens, even hundreds, of calls for fetch data to render just one web page. RavenDB client will try to batch multiple calls whenever possible and throw an exception if you cross the default threshold of 30 calls per single session. However, as you will see later, you can reduce the number of calls to one or two in most cases. This is a significant speedup for your application, and it is lowering the load on your database.

High Availability

RavenDB is an inherently distributed database. Even if you are running just one node, it will be treated as a cluster of one node. Clusters usually consist of several nodes, most commonly three. Such a multi-node setup will provide several exact copies of your database, and as long as just one node is up and running, your data will be available.

Topologies

RavenDB clusters can scale from one node to several million nodes. Your setup can include cloud hosting, local machines, and all kinds of heterogeneous arrangements. Finally, various star-shaped topologies are supported with a central location performing two-way complete or filtered replication with millions of edge locations.

How to Start?

The easiest way to start working with RavenDB is to open your browser and access `http://live-test.ravendb.net/`. What will open for you is RavenDB studio.

Figure 1-1. *RavenDB Playground Server Studio*

What you are now looking at in Figure 1-1 is RavenDB studio, a web application for managing your RavenDB server. As you can see, there is no need to install anything – your server is providing you with a web application accessible from all major web browsers.

Playground Server is a public instance of RavenDB, open for everyone without a need to authenticate. You can create new databases, play around with them, and evaluate how RavenDB works.

Caution   Do not use Playground Server for anything but evaluation of RavenDB. Do not store any sensitive data in any of the databases. They are unprotected and open for anyone in the world to access, see all the databases, and read and modify data. Also, all databases are wiped out periodically.

The easiest way to run RavenDB from your machine is Docker. If you already have it on your machine, all you have to do is to run the following command:

```
docker run -d -p 8080:8080 -p 38888:38888 -e RAVEN_ARGS="--Setup.Mode=
None --License.Eula.Accepted=true" ravendb/ravendb
```

Docker will fetch the latest RavenDB image and will spin up a new container to run this image. Now, if you open `http://127.0.0.1:8080/`, you will see Studio in your browser.

18

Note   You are now running RavenDB in developer mode. There is no authentication nor authorization enforced. Developer mode is the only situation when RavenDB will allow unauthenticated access.

You can also run RavenDB natively on Windows, Linux, OSX, and even Raspberry Pi. For example, to set up RavenDB on a Windows machine, go to `https://ravendb.net/download`, select "Windows 64" platform, and download zip archive. After unpacking an archive, execute `run.ps1` file and you will start RavenDB.

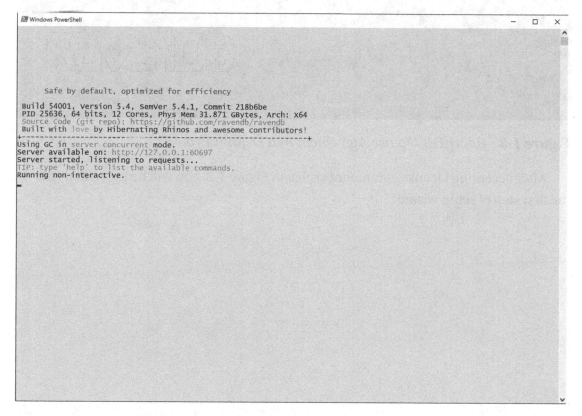

Figure 1-2. *RavenDB PowerShell Console in Windows*

As shown in Figure 1-2, the server will run on IP address 127.0.0.1, and the default browser will open with RavenDB End-User License Agreement.

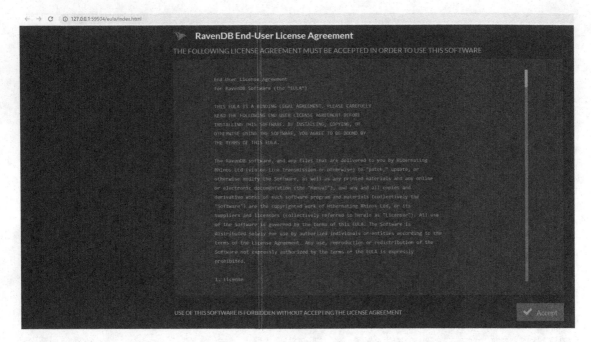

Figure 1-3. *RavenDB License Agreement in a Default Browser*

After accepting License Agreement visible in Figure 1-3, you will be presented with the first step of setup wizard.

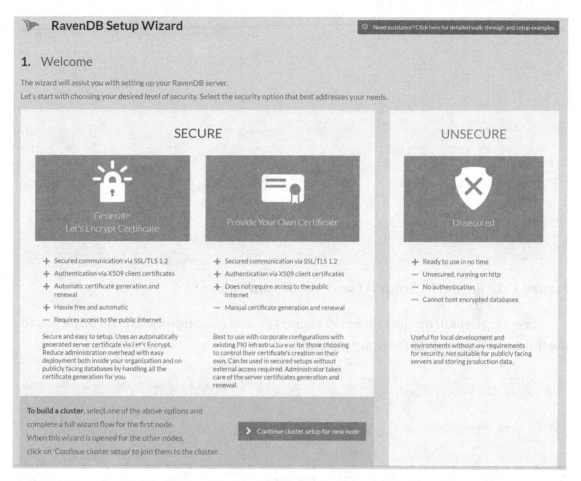

Figure 1-4. *RavenDB Setup Wizard, the First Step*

Since you will be running a local instance for development purposes, you can select "Unsecure" mode, as shown in Figure 1-4. This will lead you to the second step of the setup wizard – Unsecure Mode Setup.

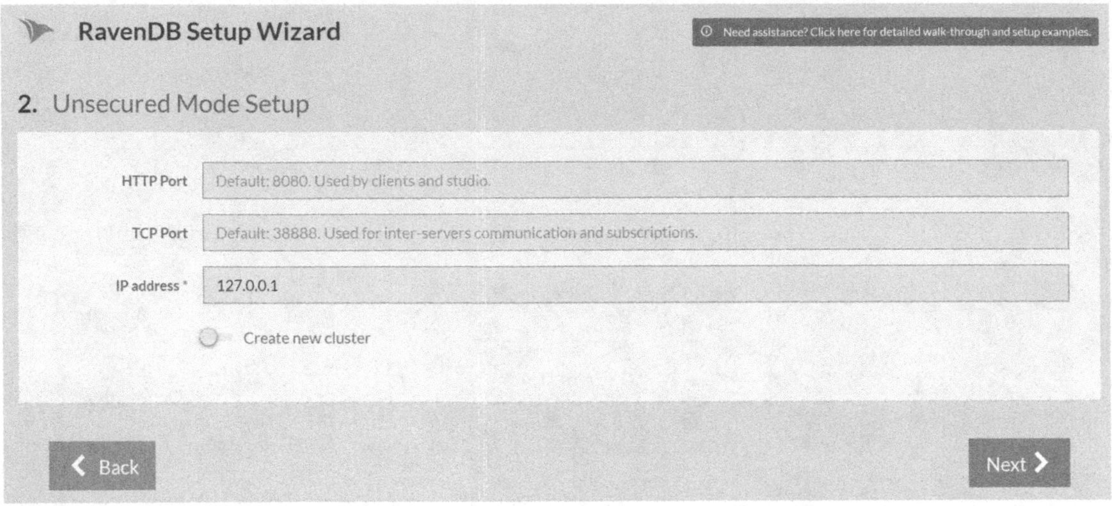

Figure 1-5. *RavenDB Setup Wizard, the Second Step*

Accepting default options shown in Figure 1-5, and clicking on *Next* will bring you to the third and final step of the setup procedure.

Figure 1-6. *RavenDB Setup Wizard, the Third and Final Step*

There is just one step, shown in Figure 1-6, needed before you can start working with your local instance of RavenDB under Windows. Clicking on the *Restart server* button will restart the server and reload your browser window. Finally, `http://127.0.0.1:8080/studio/index.html` will open, and you will see the same screen from Figure 1-1.

Creating Your First Database

Now that you have the RavenDB server up and running, it is time to create your first database. First, click on the *Databases* option in the left column of Studio. You will see a notification that there are no databases, along with a call to action to create one. You can also create a new database by clicking on a *New database* in the upper right corner, visible in Figure 1-7.

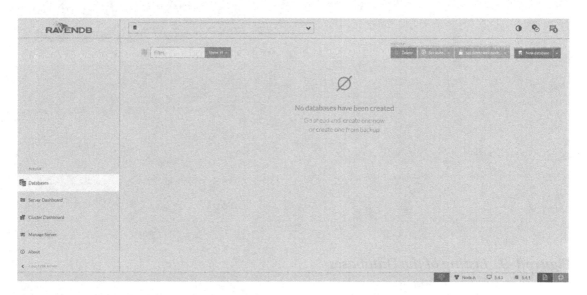

Figure 1-7. *Creating New Database*

This will bring up *New database* dialog.

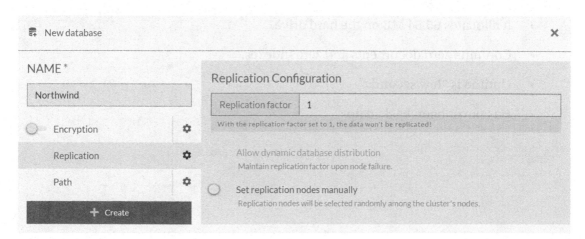

Figure 1-8. *New Database Dialog*

At this point, as shown in Figure 1-8, all you need to do is to enter the name of the new database and click on *Create* button. Name your new database Northwind, accept all defaults, and new empty database will be created.

You are now back to the same Databases screen you started from, but this time, you can see the Northwind database you just created, as shown in Figure 1-9.

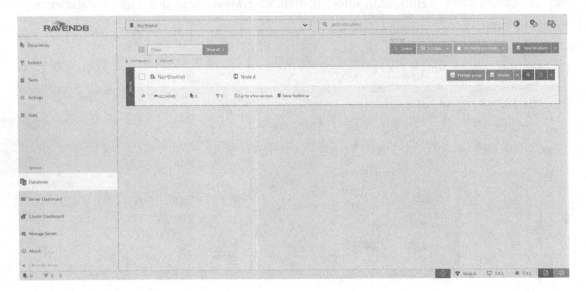

Figure 1-9. *Listing of the Databases*

Looking more closely at Figure 1-10, you can see basic information about your new database:

- Residing on Node A.

- It allocates 65.54 MB on the hard drive.

- Contains zero documents and zero indexes.

- Uptime is "few seconds."

- Has never been backed up.

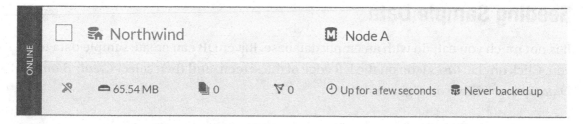

Figure 1-10. *Basic Database Info*

Clicking on a database name *Northwind* opens a list of documents, and you will see that your database is empty indeed, as visible on Figure 1 11.

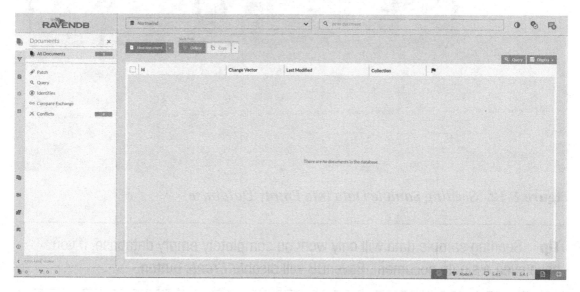

Figure 1-11. *An Empty List of Documents in the Database*

Seeding Sample Data

It is not much you can do with an empty database. RavenDB can create sample data for you. Click on the *Tasks* icon on the left edge of the screen, and then select *Create Sample Data* option, visible on Figure 1-12.

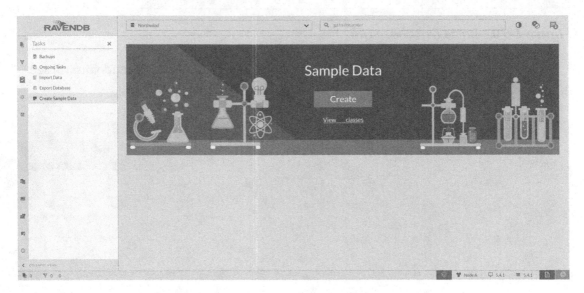

Figure 1-12. *Seeding Sample Data into Empty Database*

Tip   Seeding sample data will only work on completely empty database. If you have even a single document, RavenDB will disable *Create* button.

Northwind Database

Going back to the Documents menu item reveals documents and collections, as you can see in Figure 1-13.

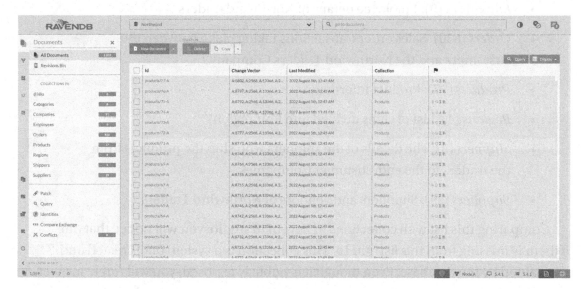

Figure 1-13. *Collections and Documents in the Northwind Database*

Collections are one of the basic concepts in RavenDB. They contain documents and are very similar to tables in relational databases. However, there are no requirements for documents in one collection to have identical structures or any schema. Every document belongs to exactly one collection, and you will usually group similar documents in one collection.

The database in front of you is *Northwind*. It is one of the sample databases Microsoft is shipping with Access and SQL Server applications. Since 1994, it has been used as a basis for tutorials and demonstrations of various features in various database products. The wider community accepted it as an excellent tutorial schema for a small business ERP, and it has been ported to a variety of non-Microsoft databases, including PostgreSQL. Hence, the choice of this data as a sample in RavenDB was a logical one. There is a high probability that an average user is already familiar with a relational version.

The Northwind database contains the sales data for a fictitious company called "Northwind Traders," which imports and exports specialty foods worldwide.

The dataset includes sample data for the following:

- *Categories* (8 documents): Product categories

- *Companies* (91): Customers who buy products from Northwind

- *Employees* (9): Employee details of Northwind traders

- *Orders* (830): Sales order transactions taking place between the customers and the Northwind Traders Company

- *Products* (77): Product information

- *Regions* (4): List of cities divided into four regions

- *Shippers* (3): The details of the shippers who ship the products from the traders to the end-customer Companies

- *Suppliers* (29): Suppliers and vendors of Northwind Traders

Comparing this list with collections in RavenDB studio, you will notice that one of them is missing from this list: @hilo. This collection is a system one, created and maintained by the database. Even though it is publicly exposed, you will rarely inspect its content. Documents you can see inside are used to create unique identifiers for documents in your collections. Also, pay attention to a specific prefix of this collection; its name starts with the "at" sign. This prefix is a standard convention for all properties and names used internally by RavenDB. Even though nothing stops you from naming your properties using the same prefix, we recommend you avoid this to prevent any conflict with system names.

Documents

Click on the *Orders* collection, and you will get a listing of all documents in this collection. Now, following Figure 1-14, click on *Id* `orders/830-A` to open your first RavenDB document.

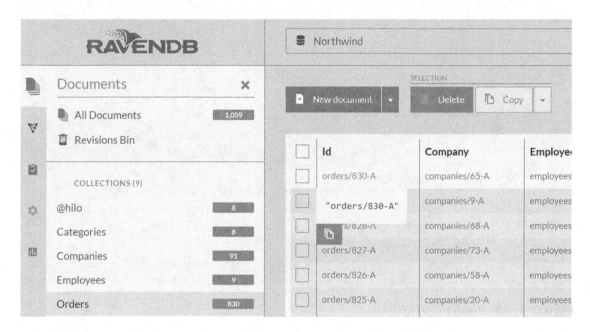

Figure 1-14. *Documents in the Orders Collection*

You are now looking at JSON document stored in the Northwind database, as shown in Figure 1-15.

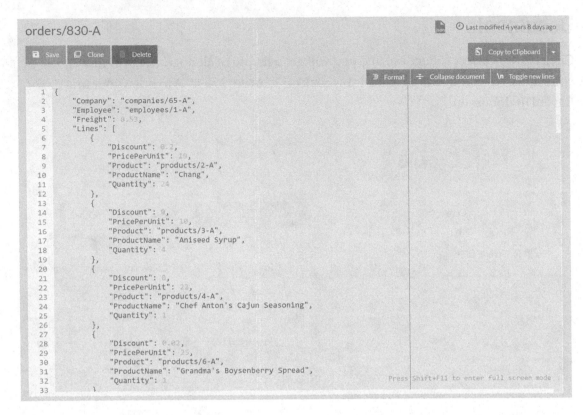

Figure 1-15. *JSON Document*

If you have been working with relational databases, this is not a familiar sight. There are no columns. The whole document is one JSON structure. *Lines* property is an array consisting of JSON objects. Scroll down, and you will see the *ShipTo* property, which contains a complex nested JSON structure.

Comparing this document to the usual RDBMS modeling, you will find out that we did not have to split it into several pieces to satisfy the tabular nature of relational databases. *Company* and *Employee* properties, for example, are references to other documents in this database, but they are not special properties – they are just simple strings.

Document-based modeling is an important topic which we will cover in more detail in the following chapters. For now, feel free to click on other collections and inspect their documents.

Summary

In this chapter, we briefly covered the history of relational databases and their inception, advantages, and some shortcomings of these systems. As a next step in the evolution of data persistence, NoSQL databases emerged. We went over the motivation for creating this new class of databases, some problems they are solving, and their main categories. RavenDB was introduced, and we covered installation steps, creation of your first database, an overview of the sample dataset, and the very concept of JSON documents.

In the next chapter, we will show the data modeling approach with NoSQL document databases, explaining how you can apply them in RavenDB. Additionally, we will also cover techniques for modeling NoSQL document relationships.

CHAPTER 2

Document Modeling

Modeling is the critical process at the heart of every application development. We could easily dedicate a whole book to this topic, so devoting just one chapter to this topic inevitably leads to many omissions. However, our goal here is to give you a brief introduction to the process of modeling and factors affecting it and to explain a document-based approach.

In this chapter, we will first look into the conceptual overview of modeling. After that, we will remind ourselves how we model data in relational databases, what affects this process, and what limitations are. Next, we will look into the document-based modeling approach, the ideas behind this concept, and its main characteristics. After that, we will address some common doubts you might have during a transition period from relational modeling to document-based modeling. Finally, you will see standard techniques to model relationships between documents in the NoSQL database.

Abstraction and Generalization

The British statistician George E. P. Box famously said, "All models are wrong, but some are useful." This statement is true not only for mathematics and statistics but in every situation where we need to describe reality. From building mental models for understanding life events to writing invoice-processing applications in C#, you will always need to create a representation of reality.

Software developers are writing computer programs that describe a particular domain of life and enable users to track real-life entities, their relations, and various ways in which these entities are affecting each other. In reality, environments are not *simple* (consisting of few objects) but usually *complex* (many components).

Also, the reality is not intuitive (easy to grasp) but *complicated*. In such systems, connections and interactions between objects are not obvious. Many moving parts are highly interconnected. Consequentially, every change that happens to one or more

© Dejan Miličić 2022
D. Miličić, *Introducing RavenDB*, https://doi.org/10.1007/978-1-4842-8919-8_2

entities affects them and is also propagating through the rest of the system. This rippling effect is hard to grasp, and those unforeseen consequences of changes are hard to understand and tame and describe in a programming language.

Luckily, software developers are not helpless when faced with these challenges, and there are many tools and approaches we developed over the years. One of the most important ones is an *abstraction*. We will narrow our scope to the subdomain that only covers entities we are interested in when modeling. Furthermore, we will look at the properties of these entities and isolate major ones, ignoring all details which are not contributing to the representation of our subdomain. This process is at the heart of *abstraction* – removing various information that are not contributing to our understanding of the subdomain we are modeling. We can say that this is very similar to the process of *generalization* – selecting a specific group of objects, observing their common or shared properties, and then using these properties to describe them.

For example, imagine that we are building an application for a small neighborhood bookstore. The bookstore owner intends to create a members club for customers. They could join in, populate their areas of interest and basic personal information, and receive weekly reading recommendations, exclusive discounts, and alerts about new arrivals of interest. Faced with the challenge of building such a service, you would first understand the domain, users, interactions between them, and outcomes your application would have to produce. Next, you would approach modeling of all identified entities in the system.

Looking at just one of these entities – customer – reveals an almost endless set of details about them. Customers have first and last names, email addresses, and dates of birth. But they also have eye color, favorite perfume, and favorite restaurant. Coming back to our goal, which is building a book recommendation service, will reveal which of these customer attributes are helpful for our effort and which ones we can ignore. After a short conversation with a bookstore owner, we conclude that eye color, perfume, and restaurant choice are not affecting book choice, and we decide to omit them from our model.

We can repeatedly apply this mental process to remove one by one any attributes irrelevant to our goal. Any model property that is not contributing to our intention will be removed, resulting in the simplification of our model. This way, our application will contain only relevant data, which will have a narrow scope. Less data means a simpler (less complex) model, and it will result in less complicated processes we need to implement. Interestingly, when modeling, we will reach a better outcome if we ignore the attributes of entities. Hence, a less precise and less comprehensive model will be better in describing our domain and serving the needs of our application.

Also, we must be aware that the software we are building and the models we are creating are not the goals by themselves. Models are means for supporting our users. Hence, as real life and circumstances are evolving, we should also develop, modify, and expand our applications to support these changes. Our models should describe the present state and support processes occurring at the initial phase of building application. Still, they must also be sustainable to modifications to support changes with reasonable effort from our side. Domains will expand, unexpected things will happen in life, and our model will inevitably evolve with it to keep these changes.

Modeling in Relational Databases

A data model is a collection of structures and shapes to describe and manipulate our data. During the dominance of relational databases, the dominant data model was the relational data model (RDM). It consists of a set of tables, with each table holding a collection of rows. Every row represents an entity that is composed of columns (cells). A column may contain a reference to a row in the same or some other table, implementing the concept of the relationship between two entities.

Let's look at a straightforward example of data model. Figure 2-1 shows a purchase order document.

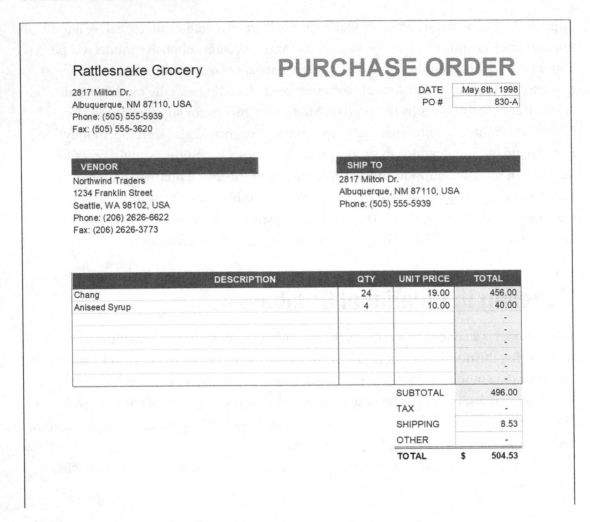

Rattlesnake Grocery

2817 Milton Dr.
Albuquerque, NM 87110, USA
Phone: (505) 555-5939
Fax: (505) 555-3620

PURCHASE ORDER

DATE	May 6th, 1998
PO #	830-A

VENDOR	SHIP TO
Northwind Traders	2817 Milton Dr.
1234 Franklin Street	Albuquerque, NM 87110, USA
Seattle, WA 98102, USA	Phone: (505) 555-5939
Phone: (206) 2626-6622	
Fax: (206) 2626-3773	

DESCRIPTION	QTY	UNIT PRICE	TOTAL
Chang	24	19.00	456.00
Aniseed Syrup	4	10.00	40.00
			-
			-
			-
			-
			-

SUBTOTAL	496.00
TAX	-
SHIPPING	8.53
OTHER	-
TOTAL	$ 504.53

Figure 2-1. *Purchase Order Document*

Figure 2-2 is showing a typical relational data model. There are two entities which can translate to tables. The orders entity contains one row per order, and the order_lines entity holds one row per line item.

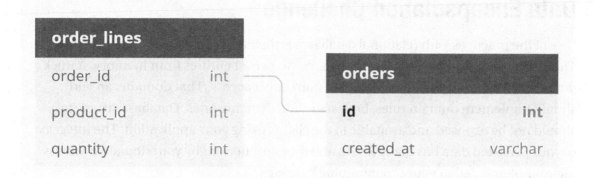

Figure 2-2. *Relational Database Model for Order*

As you can see, this relational database model provides us with the means to store order documents. Every row is a collection of simple values. Rows are incapable of representing anything complex – you cannot store lists or nested structures. For that reason, we could not keep order lines which are an integral part of the Order. In order words, lack of advanced capabilities forced us to split complex entities like Order into two tables: orders and order_lines.

As we have just seen, RDBMS tables are very similar to Excel sheets – row after row of cells, containing simple linear information – like the number, string, or date. Order row cannot persist the list of Order Lines, so we had to introduce one more table to hold Order Lines and establish a relationship between these two tables to denote parent-child connection.

Looking at the modeling exercise on this ordinary document revealed three things that we had to do:

1. Create table orders.

2. Create table order_lines.

3. Define ownership connection between these two tables.

We started with a document that exists as a single sheet of paper in real life. To model this paper document in our relational database, we have to create two entities and establish a connection. This separation of Order from its Lines is forced upon us by the technical limitations of the RDBMS itself.

Data Encapsulation Challenge

One of the practices with relational databases is their overexposure to direct access. The database should be looked upon as a way to persist entities from memory. A thick domain layer should shield the database from direct access. That domain can and should implement domain rules, both static and dynamic ones. Database structure should not be exposed and available to the clients using your application. The integrity of your persisted data has many levels, and they are checked by your domain business logic, implemented in your programming language.

Modeling in NoSQL Databases

This section will look at the genesis of the modeling approach with NoSQL databases, techniques that can represent your data, and some of the best practices.

Looking at programming languages, you can express your ideas in any language – it is possible, indeed, to develop an ERP system in assembly. But assembly is not the best tool for that task – as years passed, our industry developed better tools for developing business applications.

The same goes with databases – you can model the same domain in relational databases and NoSQL/document databases. There are no technical limitations. However, many developers will find document-oriented modeling as more natural compared to relational modeling. Document-oriented models are closer to real-life documents that are modeled, and you need to make fewer adjustments than dictated by the technical aspects of your database.

Your habits will be the single biggest obstacle when working with document databases. Over the years, if not decades, you were doing things in one manner, and now, all of a sudden, you need to give up, forget about all the best practices, and start following a new set of best practices in a leap of faith.

Relational databases are based on tables and relationships between them. And, when modeling for RDBMS, you are following that. We can model everything as a set of tables in a relational database, but that same thing can also be modeled as a document in the NoSQL database. The real challenge is creating a model that would enable you to leverage features offered by the concrete database you are using. A suitable and appropriate document data model can make your life easier and make you almost completely forget about the database – your database can become a "boring" component of your development cycle.

So, the first rule of good document-oriented modeling is "Do not apply relational database modeling techniques to NoSQL." Relational and Document databases are two different worlds. They apply different paradigms, have different approaches, and have completely different philosophies.

If you fail to follow this advice, you will end up with an inappropriate and suboptimal model. That can make your life harder and make you fight your database even with simple tasks. However, you should treat your database not as your enemy. It would help if you treated it as your ally and friend. And friends are there to help.

JSON Documents

The first essential characteristic of NoSQL document databases is the format in which they are storing documents. For most NoSQL databases, JSON is either a native or supported format. Specified in the early 2000s by Douglas Crockford, JSON stands for JavaScript Object Notation. This format is textual, standardized by ECMA, and even though it is a subset of JavaScript, JSON is language-independent.

Returning to our example of Order with Order Lines, we can represent it in JSON format in the following way:

```
{
  "Company": "ACME",
  "Total": 496,
  "Lines": [
    {
        "ProductName": "Chang",
        "PricePerUnit": 19,
        "Quantity": 24
    },
    {
        "ProductName": "Aniseed Syrup",
        "PricePerUnit": 10,
        "Quantity": 4
    }
  ]
}
```

Unlike relational databases, we do not have technical limitations forcing us to split this Order into multiple entities. Furthermore, JSON is an industry-standard format for data exchange. All major languages like C#, Java, or Python support serialization of objects to JSON format and deserialization from JSON back to objects.

Hence, when modeling the data domain for a NoSQL database, our goal is to develop a set of JSON documents describing our subdomain. In the next section, we will see how to approach this nontrivial task.

Properties of Well-Modeled Documents

There is no algorithm you could apply to reach a perfect model. Modeling skills are gained through experience over many projects. You will attempt to produce a model, implement it, and then evaluate it over time, as your application is working and as change requests are arriving. Also, there is never just one way to model things. There are many variants, and you can never label any of the variants as "proper," "best," "most appropriate," or "by the book." Many factors will affect this process – you will have to think about performance, storage allocation, type of queries, business rules, and directions. Your application will most likely evolve.

However, even though we cannot develop strict rules and recipes for shaping and structuring documents, we can observe some good properties of well-modeled documents. Years of modeling experience taught us what desired properties are:

- *Independent*: Document should have its separate existence from any other documents.

- *Isolated*: Document should be able to change independently from other documents.

- *Coherent*: Document should be legible on its own without referencing other documents.

The benefits of these desired outcomes can be easiest explained by showing the consequences of modeling, which would not respect these principles. Let's look one more time (in Listing 2-1) at our JSON model from the previous section.

Listing 2-1. JSON Order Document

```json
{
  "Company": "ACME",
  "Total": 496,
  "Lines": [
    {
      "ProductName": "Chang",
      "PricePerUnit": 19,
      "Quantity": 24
    },
    {

      "ProductName": "Aniseed Syrup",
      "PricePerUnit": 10,
      "Quantity": 4
    }
  ]
}
```

Listing 2-1 shows the JSON representation of an order. As you can see, this order has two order lines. Observe the first one:

```json
{

    "ProductName": "Chang",
    "PricePerUnit": 19,
    "Quantity": 24
}
```

Now, let us consider if we can model this order line as a separate document from the perspective of our first goal – *independence*. Is this order line independent? Can it have meaningful existence? Thinking further, have you ever seen an order line printed on paper, without any more details? The answer is clear – the order line cannot have an independent existence; it does not have a meaning outside of the scope of its parent Order. We were modeling Order Line as a separate document that would result in JSON depleted of the substance.

Next, let us examine the level of isolation our Order has compared to other documents in the system. The Document is not *isolated* if updating it also means you need to update any other documents in your database. So we can ask a question - are any changes in the content of this Order affecting products or the Company? The answer is not. Hence, we validated that our model for the order respects principle of *isolation*. Approaching this from the perspective of negating this principle, here would be an example of the Order model that would not be isolated:

```
{
  "Company": {
    "Name": "ACME",
    "TotalOrders": 1,
  }
  "Total": 496,
  "Lines": [
    {
        "ProductName": "Chang",
        "PricePerUnit": 19,
        "Quantity": 24
    },
    {
        "ProductName": "Aniseed Syrup",
        "PricePerUnit": 10,
        "Quantity": 4
    }
  ]
}
```

In this example, we decided to expand company info to keep track of total orders. Consequently, every time we create a new Order, we need to update all existing orders for the same Company and increase TotalOrders value by one. Such an expanded model is not isolated anymore. Changes we make within one Document's scope generate the ripple effect, resulting in a mandatory change to one or more other documents.

Finally, if the Document is not *coherent*, it would not be possible to establish its meaning based solely on the information it contains. Examining our Order, we can conclude that we have all information we need: Acme Company made an Order of multiple quantities of two products; we can see what prices we promised to them and the total value of this Order. However, upon closer examination, we realize that we do not know where to deliver ordered goods. We need to reach one more Document containing the Acme address, to gain complete information about this Order. Here is how we can expand our Order model to make it coherent:

```
{
  "Company": "ACME",
  "ShippingAddress": {
      "City": "Albuquerque",
      "Country": "USA",
      "Line1": "2817 Milton Dr."
  },
  "Total": 496,
  "Lines": [
    {
        "ProductName": "Chang",
        "PricePerUnit": 19,
        "Quantity": 24
    },
    {

        "ProductName": "Aniseed Syrup",
        "PricePerUnit": 10,
        "Quantity": 4
    }
  ]
}
```

In this section, we learned what the three properties of well-modeled documents are. After that, we checked our initial Order model against these principles and finally corrected our initial model into the final version. This final Order document holds complete information about the Order (*coherence*), and any changes we make to it will not force us to update other documents (*isolation*). Also, the *independent* nature of this model provides us with the freedom to produce a paper version and send it within the envelope – the recipient will be able to examine and understand it without the need to ask additional questions.

We managed to achieve one more aspect with this modeling – we created a *temporal snapshot* model. Our Document captures all relevant information as they were at the time of document creation. For example, we recorded prices for both of the products – if these products become cheaper or more expensive after the creation of the Order, that change will not affect our Document. Also, the shipment address is verified to be a valid one. If it changes in the future, e.g., if Company relocates, we will have a precise record that the shipment went to Albuquerque, USA, and not some other city or country. The importance of this data corruption prevention cannot be understated.

In the next section, we will see that besides these properties of quality models, we also have one more powerful mental model for the development of document models.

Aggregates

As we saw in the previous chapter, the NoSQL ecosystem has many different flavors and approaches implemented by various databases. However, three categories – key-value, document, and column-family store – share a common approach by providing you with the ability to define *aggregates*.

Aggregate is a term originating in domain-driven design (DDD), where it represents a collection of related objects treated as one single unit. Suppose you think about the separation of your paper document into information pieces as an act of normalization. In that case, Aggregate orientation represents the opposite process - *denormalization* - deciding which of these separated chunks of data belong together and bringing them together into one unit.

A natural question that follows is "how big and comprehensive this unit should be"? If the third normal form is one extreme, shall we go to the other extreme and model the whole domain as one large unit? To answer this question, we need to look into the gist of what aggregate as a unit represents.

Unit of Change and Unit of Consistency

An aggregate is a *unit of change* and a *unit of consistency*.

A *unit of change* will be every entity in your database model that can handle all requested changes without a need to go to other documents. In other words, changes we make are propagating within one aggregate.

Going back to our three properties of well-modeled documents, we can see that aggregates are as follows:

- Independent and coherent – they are a collection of related objects joined together in one Document. These objects are containing complete and rounded information and can exist as a separate unit. We can understand an aggregate without a need to look into related aggregates.

- Isolated – as a unit of change, aggregates can be modified independently of other documents.

The second important property of an aggregate is that they represent a *unit of consistency*. A consistent database will, at any point in time, contain only valid data. All information stored in a database will conform to all business rules, constraints, and validation checks. No matter what changes we apply to our aggregates, if we use our validation rules, they will remain valid when saved to the database.

Going back to our ubiquitous Order example, if we add one more line to the Lines collection, we also need to update the `Total` property by recalculating the new total value of our Order. If it contains some more properties, like VAT or shipping costs, they will need to be updated. The system we are building can have some more advanced rules – e.g., we might offer a volume discount for shipping overseas. In that case, adding just one more order line will trigger a set of updates, rule checks, validation checks, and some more updates resulting from various calculations. After applying all updates, we will persist Order in the database in an atomic manner; our Order aggregate contains a set of units that changed together. This changeset was validated to conform to all business and other validation rules. We are now sure that our database holds Order that contains only valid data.

Distributed Systems

However, a database is just one component of the software system we are building. Taking a broader look, we will see that modern applications are complex. They consist of many components, coming in various forms – from utility classes, over in-process services to physically separated services and executing across a network of interconnected machines. Services are communicating synchronously or asynchronously.

As an example, look at a simple webshop. Customers can add products to the shopping cart and complete Orders. Order is saved in the webshop application, a confirmation email is sent, and the Order is pushed to the ERP system at the core of operations. Even with this small system, we can see three major separated components:

– Webshop application

– Email server

– ERP system

These are three isolated components existing on separated machines, communicating over the network. A system composed in this way is considered to be a *distributed system*.

Sending confirmation email, creating a new Order, and pushing it into the ERP system are one transactional operation from the perspective of your business logic. However, in a distributed system like this one is, the standard notion of transaction you are used to does not apply anymore. For example, what happens if the ERP system is not available when you try to send it new Order? Shall you abandon it? In that scenario, when will we send a confirmation email?

Distributed systems are challenging because they are complex and because many assumptions you usually make do not hold anymore. Operations you were executing as synchronous ones before might be asynchronous in the distributed system. Each time you communicate over the network, you must provide a fallback for the scenario of communication failure. Messages sent between distributed components will sometimes be queued and delivered dozens of seconds, maybe even minutes after you initially send them.

As a result, in most cases, in distributed systems, you will not be able to count on the transactional nature of your applications. Distributed systems have a notion of *eventual consistency*. Your business transaction will eventually complete, but there are no guarantees how long it will take for changes you ordered to be delivered and accepted by the components of the system. At the end of this propagation process, your distributed system will become consistent, but this fact is something that you must be aware of all the time.

Aggregates in the Distributed System

Revisiting the notion of the *aggregate* in the context of distributed systems reveals a significant impact on the design of aggregate boundaries. Namely, the scope of aggregate boundaries will determine units of data that will be part of it. Coming back to the fact that an aggregate is a *unit of change* and a *unit of consistency*, we can conclude that modifying and saving aggregate into the database will represent one *transaction.*

What is a transaction? The transaction represents an individual indivisible operation that either succeeds or fails as a complete unit. Partial completeness of the transaction is not possible, and when transaction processing is finished, you will have precise and reliable feedback about the outcome. This property is usually called *atomicity*, precisely because of the indivisible nature of the transaction.

Why is atomicity important? The transaction usually represents a group of tightly coupled operations. Executing only some of them might bring your data into an inconsistent and corrupted state. As an example, imagine adding a new product to the Order. You will

- Create a new order line with a product.

- Recalculate order total to include the amount of new order line.

What would happen if just one of these two operations is executed? You would either charge for a product that would not be included in the Order or have the product in the Order without increasing the Total. In other words, you would either create financial damage to yourself or your customer.

Hence, it is clear that we need to treat both of these operations as one atomic unit. As a result, both of them will succeed (new order line is created and Total is correctly updated), or both fail (order total remains the same since no new order lines were added). Transaction failure is nothing dramatic per se. You can handle it in several standard ways, including retrying it, before showing an error message. However, what is essential is that in both cases of successful or unsuccessful outcomes, your data will remain in a consistent state.

Aggregates as Transaction Boundaries

We can conclude that aggregates are supporting transactions. We will load a Document that represents aggregate, update it, and save it back to the database in a transactional manner on a database level, which results in a guarantee of consistency of our Document.

You can ask yourself – why can we not update two documents in one transaction? This is possible indeed. As we already mentioned, modeling is a subtle intellectual activity. There are no complex rules, and everything you read so far is a recommendation based on best practices learned through the practical application of these principles. So, updating two aggregate documents in one transaction is possible. However, recommended approach would be to group things that change together transactionally into one aggregate and then propagate changes through the rest of the system in an eventually consistent manner. Also, on many occasions, you will be forced by the nature of your distributed system to go with eventual consistency.

One typical example would be a separation of your application into microservices. Every microservice will usually have its database. Transactions that are spanning two or more aggregates hosted within different databases are unviable and hard. This approach will create more problems than benefits for you as you develop, maintain, and evolve such application.

Hence, it would help if you looked at the boundaries of your aggregate as transactional boundaries. For most of the changes in your application, you will have to load, change, and save just one Document – a document that represents your aggregate.

Everything else that happens in your system will not be transactional but eventually consistent. You should take this into account and implement error handling mechanisms. Also, you should carefully approach every single business scenario in your application and determine when synchronous communication is a must and when you can use asynchronous communication.

Modeling in RavenDB

This section will show how RavenDB handles documents and how you can create and inspect documents. Also, we will take a look at identifiers assigned to each RavenDB document.

Documents

RavenDB is storing documents in JSON format, and they are almost unlimited in size – they can grow up to 2Gb. However, you should limit the size of your documents to be no bigger than a couple of megabytes. JSON larger than that is cumbersome to load and save back into the database and is a usually strong signal that your model is suboptimal.

In the previous chapter, we created an empty database and seeded it with some sample data. In Figure 2-3, you can see one Order document from the Orders collection.

```
orders/830-A

  Save      Clone      Delete

 1  {
 2      "Company": "companies/65-A",
 3      "Employee": "employees/1-A",
 4      "Freight": 8.53,
 5      "Lines": [
 6          {
 7              "Discount": 0.2,
 8              "PricePerUnit": 19,
 9              "Product": "products/2-A",
10              "ProductName": "Chang",
11              "Quantity": 24
12          },
13          {
14              "Discount": 0,
15              "PricePerUnit": 10,
16              "Product": "products/3-A",
17              "ProductName": "Aniseed Syrup",
18              "Quantity": 4
19          },
20          {
21              "Discount": 0,
22              "PricePerUnit": 22,
23              "Product": "products/4-A",
24              "ProductName": "Chef Anton's Cajun Seasoning",
25              "Quantity": 1
26          },
27          {
28              "Discount": 0.02,
29              "PricePerUnit": 25,
30              "Product": "products/6-A",
31              "ProductName": "Grandma's Boysenberry Spread",
32              "Quantity": 1
33          },
34          {
```

Figure 2-3. Order Document in RavenDB

This document consists of two main elements:

- Identifier *orders/830-A*

- JSON body

These two are mandatory. Every RavenDB Document must have a unique identifier and non-empty JSON content.

Let's create our first Document. For the beginning, create a new empty database following directions from the previous chapter. After a database is successfully created, you will see a screen, as shown in Figure 2-4.

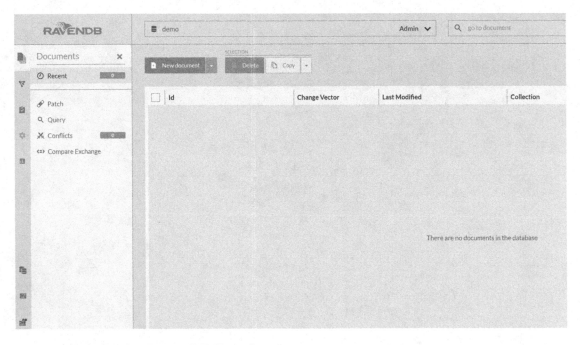

Figure 2-4. *Empty RavenDB Database*

To create a new document, you need to click on a *New document* button, which will open the screen shown in Figure 2-5.

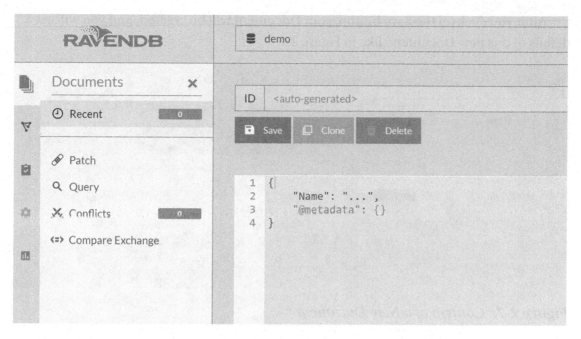

Figure 2-5. *Creation of New Document*

Populate ID field with `users/`, and for the value of field Name in JSON body, you can fill in the arbitrary string, as shown in Figure 2-6.

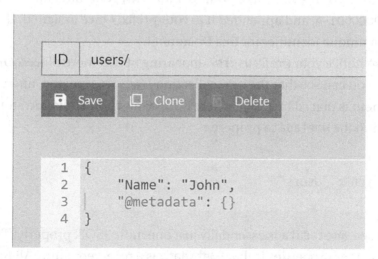

Figure 2-6. *Populating New Document*

After you click on the Save button, your Document will be created, and you will see details of this new Document, like in Figure 2-7.

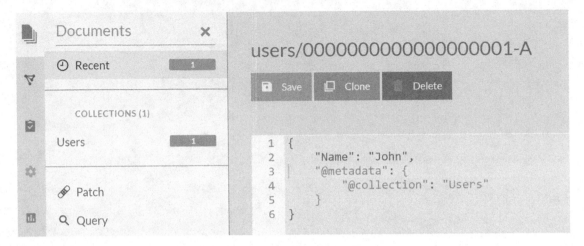

Figure 2-7. *Content of a New Document*

There are few interesting things to notice here, so let's go over each of them.

Above *Save, Clone,* and *Delete* buttons, value users/0000000000000000001-A is the ID that was generated for you. As you remember, you populated users/ in the ID field. RavenDB took this value as a prefix of future ID, generated unique suffix 0000000000000000001-A, and appended it to your prefix. Once assigned, ID cannot be changed – it is a unique identifier for this Document.

You will also notice your prefix users/ appearing in two more places. One is the left column, where you can see that the new collection *Users* was created, and your newly created Document is placed in it. But, where is this collection affiliation stored? The answer lies within the @metadata property:

```
"@metadata": {
    "@collection": "Users"
}
```

As you can see, @metadata is essentially just one more JSON property. The only difference from other properties is that @metadata is a reserved name. All RavenDB system names start with @ sign, so they will not clash with your properties. Within @metadata, property @collection contains the name of the collection.

Figure 2-5 is showing just a partial view of JSON that represents your Document. However, RavenDB Studio has functionality that you can use to inspect raw and complete JSON. As shown in Figure 2-8, in the area above your document content, there is a *Show raw output* icon.

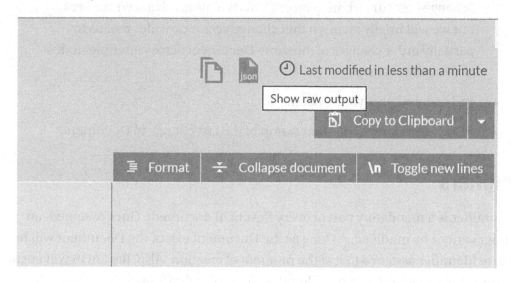

Figure 2-8. *Show Raw Output Icon*

Clicking on this icon will open new browser tab, showing complete raw JSON of your Document:

```
{
  Name: "John",
  @metadata: {
    @collection: "Users",
    @change-vector: "A:1-4Ocnef4WVEaQ9NeWn3Yhig",
    @id: "users/0000000000000000001-A",
    @last-modified: "2021-05-05T20:05:53.1467758Z"
  }
}
```

You are now able to see all system properties that @metadata contains:

- @collection - the name of the collection where your Document will be placed in.

- @change-vector – change vector. This is a more advanced concept, but we will briefly mention that change vector provides means to partially order changes of the same Document across multiple nodes in a database cluster.

- @id – identifier of your Document.

- @last-modified – UTC timestamp of the last change to Document.

Identifiers

The identifier is a mandatory part of every RavenDB document. Once assigned, an identifier cannot be modified. As long as the Document exists, the Document will have the same identifier assigned to it at the moment of creation. Also, RavenDB will ensure that every Document has a unique identifier on the database level.

Revisiting @metadata property from the previous section, we can see that @id is a string:

```
@id: "users/0000000000000000001-A"
```

When you create a new document, you can pass various string values for id, and RavenDB will react in different ways:

- Empty string – when you pass an empty string as id, RavenDB will generate a GUID and assign it as id.

- Collection_name/ – an arbitrary string followed by a forward slash. Passing users/ would be an example. The string users will be the name of the collection, and the slash will be a signal to RavenDB to generate a unique identifier for a document. This identifier will be generated as a number prepended with zeros, with the addition of the node name. For example. passing users/ as an Id for a document will result in RavenDB assigning users/0000000000000000001-A as the unique identifier.

- `Collection_name|` - arbitrary string followed by a pipe character. The arbitrary string will be taken as a name of a collection, and the pipe character will trigger cluster-wide coordination to produce a unique number on the cluster level. So, passing `users|` as an Id for a document will result in RavenDB assigning `users/1`.

- In all other cases, when a string is not empty and does not contain slash nor pipe character, RavenDB will accept it and, without modifying, assign as an id of your new Document.

If you do not have a strong reason for your IDs, it is best to let RavenDB generate IDs. Going with `collection_name/` will produce unique identifiers that will also be sortable, enabling RavenDB to store them optimally for searching and fetching. If you, for some reason, need to generate your identifiers, it is recommended to find a library that can produce lexicographically sortable identifiers.

Modeling Document Relationships

The fact that you are using a database that does not contain a *relation* in its name does not mean you will be incapable of modeling relationships between aggregates represented by documents. This section will examine possible types of relationships between documents in RavenDB, various approaches to modeling them, and how to validate stronger and weaker aspects of possible solutions.

While the previous section concentrated on the JSON content of RavenDB documents, this section is focusing on connections between those documents. These relations are not the actual data but meta-data, and the gist of modeling relations is how to expand documents to contain that additional information.

Even though there are many ways entities can be interconnected, we will look at the three most common and basic ones: one-to-one, one-to-many, and many-to-many.

One-to-One Relationship

We are mentioning this type of relationship for the first time, but you already had a chance to observe it. Let's revisit our favorite example of Order with shipping address:

```
Id: orders/1
{
  "Company": "ACME",
  "ShippingAddress": {
    "City": "Albuquerque",
    "Country": "USA",
    "Line1": "2817 Milton Dr."
  }
}
```

An order has its physical identity (usually coming in the form of a paper document) and its unique identifier orders/1. This unique identifier provides us with a means of recognizing multiple instances of the same orders – comparing two Orders comes down to comparing their Id values.

On the other hand, if we examine ShippingAddress, we will realize that it does not have an identity in the sense of distinguished unique existence. Every Order is unique, while we can have multiple shipments addressed for dispatch to the same address. To determine if two shipments are going to the exact location, we must compare all three components of our address: City, Country, Line1. Hence, we can conclude that its value represents the identity of the address. These objects are labeled as *Value Objects* in domain-driven design.

Value Object's existence is tightly coupled with their parent document. It is the only context of the entity where they are embedded, giving complete meaning to a Value Object. Let's observe one more example of a Value Object:

```
Id: users/1
{
  "Name": "John",
  "Age": 63
}
```

Imagine being presented with the number 63. What does this number represent? Someone's weight? Temperature? Hours? Price? You simply cannot tell – 63 can be so many things on its own, even a random number that does not represent anything.

Now, augmenting it with the property name, "Age": 63, we can understand it represents age. But we cannot tell who has 63 years? Maybe it's the age of a bridge or a building? Unfortunately, we lack context again.

Finally, observing this property within the entity it belongs to, we have a complete picture – John has 63 years.

This mental exercise gives us a simple recipe for recognizing Value Objects. Whenever you need a context to determine the precise meaning of the information, you will detect *Value Object (VO)*. As you saw, VO can be as simple as a number or complex structure like a shipping address, and they are fundamental building blocks of entities.

Embedding

With both *age* and *shipping address*, we applied a technique called *embedding*. Their separate existence was not justified in both cases, and we inserted these small documents inside bigger documents representing entities.

Referencing

However, there are situations where we will notice two documents, both with their own identity and justification for separate existence – and they will be in a one-to-one relationship. For example, imagine human resources management system with information about all employees within an organization. Among other things, we are keeping a Resume for every Employee – it was entered into the HRM system when the candidate applied for a position. After she accepted the offer workplace, we promoted this candidate into full-time Employee. Observing both Employee and Resume, we can see that they both have physical existence and their own identity. Also, they have a clear one-to-one relationship: every Employee has exactly one Resume, and for every Resume, we can determine an Employee who submitted it. However, before we decide how to establish a relationship, we first need to do some initial modeling. Listing 2-2 shows a model for the Employee entity.

Listing 2-2. Employee document model

```
Id: employees/1
{
  Name: "John Doe",
  DateOfBirth: "1958/05/08"
}
```

Next, we model Resume, as shown in Listing 2-3.

Listing 2-3. Resume document model

```
Id: resumes/1
{
  Employee: "employees/1",
  Education: "Yale",
  Specialty: "IT"
}
```

These two models are simplified, but they are showing basic info. Looking closely at the Resume model, we can see property Employee: "employees/1" directly linking Resume to an Employee.

This is a *reference*. References in RavenDB are nothing more than properties containing the string ID of some other document.

Since Resume is pointing to Employee with a reference, we can say this link represents *owned by* – Resume is owned by an Employee. We can reverse this relationship, as can be seen in Listing 2-4.

Listing 2-4. Employee and Resume documents with reversed reference

```
Id: employees/1
{
  Resume: "resumes/1"
  Name: "John Doe",
  DateOfBirth: "1958/05/08"
}

Id: resumes/1
{
```

```
  Education: "Yale",
  Specialty: "IT"
}
```

What we now have is Employee holding a reference to a Resume: `Resume: "resumes/1"`. This reference can be read as *owns* – Employee owns a Resume.

Of course, you can also establish a two-way one-to-one relationship, as shown in Listing 2-5.

Listing 2-5. Employee and Resume documents with mutual references

```
Id: employees/1
{
  Resume: "resumes/1",
  Name: "John Doe",
  DateOfBirth: "1958/05/08"
}
Id: resumes/1
{
  Employee: "employees/1",
  Education: "Yale",
  Specialty: "IT"
}
```

Employee and Resume are now pointing at each other via properties containing the other Document's ID. In an application displaying a screen with Employee details, we can easily offer the Resume screen because Employee holds a reference to his CV. Similarly, the screen showing Resume can offer a link leading to an accompanied Employee since we can easily access reference from the `Employee` property.

As we already mentioned, modeling is not an exact process with strict rules. What we did with Employee and Resume is that we first detected that they are related, then determined this is one-to-one relationship, and then applied three possible implementations of this relationship:

1. Unidirectional: Resume pointing to Employee.

2. Unidirectional: Employee pointing to Resume.

3. Bidirectional: Both Employee and Resume hold a reference to the other one.

However, due to the absence of technical limitations on the database level, we can also apply one more approach – embedding. We already mentioned that the relationship between Employee and Resume is one-to-one, but we also spoke about ownership. The Employee owns Resume, and Resume is owned by an Employee. This "owning" verbiage is a clear direction for embedding, as shown in Listing 2-6.

Listing 2-6. An employee with embedded Resume

```
Id: employees/1
{
  Name: "John Doe",
  DateOfBirth: "1958/05/08",
  Resume: {
    Education: "Yale",
    Specialty: "IT"
  }
}
```

In this case, we embedded not a Value Object without identity but an Entity with a clear identity. This is possible due to a clear ownership situation – Employee has exactly one Resume, and every Resume belongs to a specific Employee.

This fourth approach to modeling *one-to-one* relationships is entirely legitimate. It is up to you to examine all possible directions, think about processes and workflows in your application, and determine acceptable modeling solutions.

Also, it would be best if you thought about the future. What will be possible ways your application will evolve? What might be requests coming from your users? What will happen as the amount of data grows or if your documents are growing?

With this in mind, let's observe the modeling variant of Employee presented in Listing 2-5. For simplicity purposes, we intentionally made both Employee and Resume artificially oversimplified. However, if you recall that real-life Resumes can be pretty big, sometimes three or four pages, you will realize that you will embed a substantially extensive Document. Not only that, in the scenario where Resume contains a list of projects Employee participated in, you will see Resume growing over months and years. If you need to load, manipulate, and save Employee to the database, that means that the size of the Employee document will grow over time.

Furthermore, suppose you decide to apply same technique and embed some more documents in the same manner. In that case, you will inevitably see your Employee document becoming very large and very cumbersome to manipulate.

Finally, what will happen if requirements change and company management decided to introduce more than one Resume for every Employee – scenario where the Company applies for contracts and, as a part of a bid campaign, generates custom-tailored Resume of all project members. This will break your one-to-one modeling, which will transform into one-to-many (one Employee can have many Resumes). How much effort will it take to modify the database model and your code to accommodate this change request? Will a straightforward sentence like "we want to enable one Employee to have more than one Resume in our database" result in an inappropriately large amount of work?

All of this is showing that modeling is intricate. You will never be in a situation where you complete the model and declare it as "best possible." Hence, you should never strive for perfection and "one right way." Also, it would help if you never tried to anticipate the future and then build all variants you can foresee as a part of your domain model. What you should do instead is to make the simplest possible model that is covering present needs but also does not obstruct change requests that will be a normal and expected part of your application life cycle.

Referential Integrity in RavenDB

As you saw in the previous section, establishing references in RavenDB documents is easy. You introduce a property with a meaningful name and populate it with the referenced document's ID. From the perspective of RavenDB, there is nothing special about this property, and this is just another property with a string value. Hence, for the database engine, these two properties are structurally and functionally identical:

```
Resume: "resumes/1",
Name: "John Doe",
```

RavenDB will not check if a Resume with Id `resumes/1` exists. In the same way, you can assign an arbitrary name to your Employee, and you will be able to set the random value to your `Resume` reference:

```
Resume: "resumes/000",
Name: "Random Randomsson",
```

In this example, we created a reference to a nonexistent Resume. There was no mechanism on the database level to prevent us from introducing data corruption. Hence, it is natural to ask – relational databases were protecting us from data corruption at the database level, is this behavior exposed by RavenDB a step back? Why would I want to work with a database that is not safeguarding me from making mistakes that would corrupt my data?

Additionally, with JSON format, you will not be able to specify a type of specific property. Hence, if you have a property "age" of type integer, RavenDB will not prevent you from storing "John" in it. With a relational database, such an attempt will result in an error. So, how to explain this? Why would you go with a database that would make your application less reliable and error-prone? With a database that would let you introduce corruption in your data?

Yes, looking at the database as an isolated part of your system, that is true indeed. Relational databases like SQL Server or PostgreSQL will provide you with a way to strongly type columns and to check referential integrity, preventing you from establishing a reference to a nonexistent entity. However, observing databases in the broader context of data persistence gives a significantly different angle.

Unlike the 1980s and 1990s, today's modeling methodologies (such as domain-driven design) are not centered around databases as a starting point in the modeling process. Instead, they recommend modeling the business domain in the programming language and then persisting domain entities into the database. In the past, most planning meetings were starting in front of the whiteboard, where developers would draw relational database tables, fields, and lots of Foreign Keys establishing relationships between them. This process looked very similar to UML diagrams construction, except that the database was "center of the world" and whole systems planning started with modeling a database. Following persistence model, entities in the programming language were modeled, along with CRUD operations to manage these entities.

From the perspective of database "centrism," offloading validation to the database is something you are naturally striving for. However, as domain modeling techniques advanced and developed, we reached the present day where modeling is done at the conceptual level of Aggregates, Entities, and Value Objects. We perform analysis of the processes, divide enterprise projects into subdomains, and conduct modeling at the scope of a subdomain. This activity is performed to look purely at the business and process aspect of our subdomain, keeping in mind that artifacts of this activity will have to be eventually persisted. Nevertheless, persistence is a minor consideration, not a major one.

Every subdomain usually has its entities. And not only that – every subdomain has its own set of business rules, and entities should be validated according to these business constraints. As a general rule of thumb, a carefully crafted business domain should prevent the instantiation of invalid objects. One of the good rules is a principle that "impossible states should be irrepresentable." In other words, you can declare someone's age as an integer and offload that check to the database, but would it be correct from the perspective of the business domain to allow the creation and storing of an Employee with age -50 or zero? Data integrity mechanisms exposed by the relational database can cover just one minor part of the overall business validity of your data. A complete set of validation and data integrity rules is a vast one. It usually contains various static and dynamic constraints, often encompassing multiple different entities in various states. For example, a minor shopper should not be able to add a beer to a shopping cart.

Examining the primary role of a database, we can conclude that when you are storing entities into it, the database should provide a reliable mechanism to persist in-memory objects in a verbatim and sound way. Hence, you can look at the database as a way to mirror your object graph from memory into persistent media (usually a hard drive).

So, looking through narrow lenses, it is true that relational database is indeed capable of performing type-level and reference integrity checks, throwing errors at attempts to store invalid data. However, layers of business rules and checking mechanisms of high-level rules should be present in every reliable application. With a good software development approach, you will never let your objects exist in an invalid state.

Hence, the database should be placed at the proper position during application development – not in the center anymore, but as a persistence mechanism. Its role should be to store validated objects reliably and provide fast and reliable means to index and query such data.

One-to-Many Relationship

For this type of relationship, we will again turn to Orders, but this time, we will observe how they relate to Companies. Every Company can have one or more orders. Furthermore, we will consider modeling possibilities with benefits and constraints for every approach.

Revisiting principles of *independence, isolation,* and *coherence,* we can see that Company and Order should be modeled as separate documents. Choice of embedding all orders within Company would be a poor one – not only that Company and Order have a separate existence and change independently of each other – but growing number of orders as time goes by would mean that Company document would grow to be a huge one. Also, the existence of multiple orders in one Document would introduce concurrency problems; editing existing orders simultaneously with a creation of new one would introduce an optimistic concurrency violation problem. As you can see, this introspection process gave us enough arguments to determine with high security that embedding is a suboptimal choice. Hence, it is clear that Company and Order should be separate documents.

The next step is deciding how to establish a relationship between them. Looking back at one-to-one modeling, we can see there are two options. The first one, shown in Listing 2-7, shows a model where the Company holds a list of IDs of Order documents.

Listing 2-7. An employee with a list of order IDs

```
Id: employees/1
{
  Name: "John Doe",
  DateOfBirth: "1958/05/08",
  Orders: [
    "orders/1",
    "orders/2",
    "orders/3"
  ]
}
```

Orders property contains a list of IDs of orders that belong to the Company. Considering this as a possible solution for establishing a relationship between Company and Orders reveals several weak points:

- We gave up on embedding, among other reasons, because we envisioned a growing number of orders over time. Essentially, we have the same issue here. Imagine hundreds, if not thousands, of orders that the Company might have. That would cause Orders property to grow significantly. Manipulating a list of orders would be cumbersome and more and more difficult as time goes by.

- Loading orders for a Company would require first loading Company, process its Orders property, and fetch orders by obtained IDs. This is not a deal-breaker, but it represents unwanted complexity in our code and logic, generating additional database requests.

- As the number of orders for a Company grows, there is an ever-increasing number of reads and writes to a Company document. Over time, chances of optimistic concurrency violations grow proportionally.

You can see that we used a method of elimination to reach one last modeling option shown in Listing 2-8.

Listing 2-8. Orders pointing to a Company

```
Id: orders/1
{
  "Company": "companies/1",
  "ShippingAddress": {
    ...
  }
}

Id: orders/2
{
  "Company": "companies/1",
  "ShippingAddress": {
    ...
  }
}

Id: orders/3
{
  "Company": "companies/1",
  "ShippingAddress": {
    ...
  }
}
```

This model implements references on the side of orders. Every Order has a Company property that contains the ID of the parent Company. Let's now perform series of checks of this model:

- Companies and Orders are two separate collections. Each of them has their own identity, and they respect principles of isolation and independence.

- As the number of Orders grows over months or years, this will not affect the size of the documents.

- Performing queries to fetch all orders for a specific company does not require us to load Company document first.

As you can see, a model we reached is passing our checks. We can conclude we managed to establish a relationship between Companies and Orders that will support operations we can foresee.

In this example, we discovered one of the established principles of one-to-many modeling. It is colloquially called "smaller side reference," denoting the side of the relationship where ID references should be stored. As a general best practice, you should always start with a model where many documents will hold one reference to a single document, instead of going with one Document holding a long list of IDs to many documents.

Typical examples of this would be the following:

- Companies and Orders we just observed

- Professors and Students, with Students pointing to Professor

- Companies and Products, with Products pointing to Company

- Publishers and Books, with Books pointing to Publisher

Of course, every single situation is specific. Starting with the "smaller side" approach, we should also consider various present and future scenarios. Some possible examples of exceptions could be the following:

- Parents and children, where Parent might hold references to all Children

- Owner and Companies, with Owner pointing to Companies

- Team and Players, with Team having references to Players

Compared to relational databases, we do not have technical limitations – our relationships can point both ways. It is up to us to determine what direction we need. We can achieve this by putting things into context, thinking about what we are modeling, and also investing equal or maybe even more energy into projecting future growth of our application and databases.

Many-to-Many Relationship

Once you understand the nature of the one-to-many relationship, expanding to many-to-many is easy. Let's look at some real-life examples of many to many relationships.

- Communities and Members – each Community can have many Members, and each person can belong to many Communities.

- Grandparents and Grandchildren – Grandparent can have several Grandchildren, and each Grandchild has many Grandparents.

- Students and Courses – Students can enroll in many Courses, and each Course has many Students participants.

- Books and Authors – a Book can have many Authors, and each Author can write one or more Books.

All these relationships are modeled in the same way we modeled one-to-many: we will keep a list of IDs on the smaller side. Hence

- Member will have a list of his Community IDs since Communities can have thousands of Members.

- A child is likely to have fewer Grandparents than Grandparents grandchildren so that we will keep a list of associations on the child document.

- Courses can have hundreds of students, so we will expand Student to have a list of courses.

- Prolific authors can write dozens of books, while books usually have a few authors so that we will model a list of Author IDs as a property on a book document.

Now that we know how to model documents stored in a RavenDB database and establish relationships between them, the next chapter will show how we can query these documents.

Summary

In this chapter, we introduced general modeling principles in NoSQL document databases. After comparing NoSQL and SQL approaches, we covered the basics of JSON documents, aggregates, properties of well-modeled documents, and the concept of eventual consistency in distributed systems. Finally, specifics of RavenDB modeling were examined, showcasing identifiers, relationships, and an approach to referential integrity.

In the next chapter, we will focus on the most common operation in modern applications - querying. You will learn to perform essential functions like filtering, ordering, and paging. We will also cover more advanced topics, including projections, aggregations, and dereferencing relations.

CHAPTER 3

Querying

Most modern web applications perform a relatively small number of writes but a large number of reads. This chapter will look into the most common activity your application will perform and how RavenDB supports it. We will learn the basics of Raven Query Language and the basics of querying using it.

Querying in RavenDB Studio

RavenDB Studio has a dedicated panel for running queries. To reach it, open *Documents* area where all collections are listed. Below them, as visible in Figure 3-1, there are additional options. You will find *Query* as a second one.

© Dejan Miličić 2022
D. Miličić, *Introducing RavenDB*, https://doi.org/10.1007/978-1-4842-8919-8_3

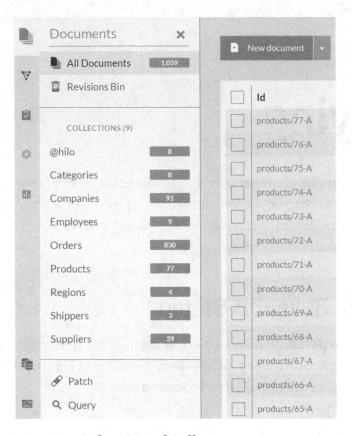

Figure 3-1. *Query Option Below List of Collections*

After you click on this menu option, you will be presented with a panel for running queries within Studio, shown in Figure 3-2.

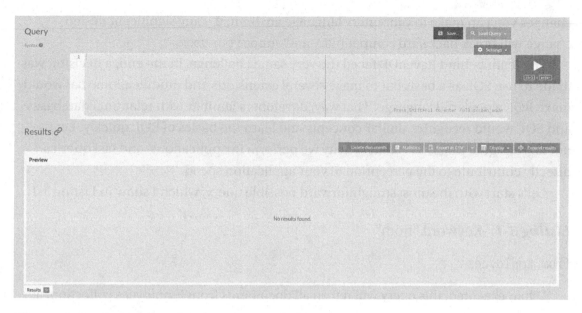

Figure 3-2. *Query Panel in RavenDB Studio*

As you can see, this panel has two fields – the upper one where you write your queries and the lower one where the result of the query execution is displayed.

After you write a query, you can run it by pressing ctrl+enter on your keyboard or clicking on the *Play* button to the right.

The following section will look into the basics of querying with Raven Query Language.

RavenDB Query Language Basics

Raven Query Language or RQL is a SQL-like query language of RavenDB. Chapter 1 mentioned that relational databases share a standardized query language called Structured Query Language - SQL. This common declarative language was one of the significant success factors for RDBMS.

Compared to that, NoSQL databases do not have standardized query language. Considering the dynamic and decentralized nature of the NoSQL ecosystem, there is a low chance any standard will ever emerge. Hence, every time a new NoSQL database is incepted, authors have the tedious task of coming up with a query language for their database. And this assignment brings a heavy burden – once you decide and create language, developers will start using it to build applications. From that point onward, changes you can make to your query language are limited – any significant design change will break backward compatibility and annoy your users.

The team behind RavenDB faced the very same challenge. In the end, a decision was made to use SQL as a basis but to make several extensions and modifications that would make RQL a powerful language. That way, developers familiar with relational databases and SQL would recognize similar concepts and learn the basics of RQL quickly. Let us not forget – querying is the main activity we perform in applications, and fast queries directly contribute to the perception of your application speed.

Let's start with the most straightforward possible query, which I show in Listing 3-1.

Listing 3-1. Keyword "from"

```
from Employees
```

When executed, this query will return all documents from Employees collection, as shown in Figure 3-3.

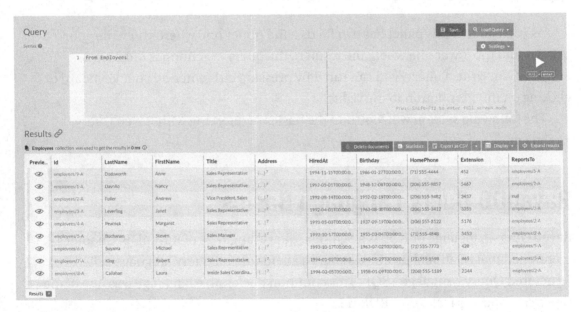

Figure 3-3. *Selecting All Documents from Employees Collection*

You can see results in a table, but this is just a visual presentation. Each row is showing one JSON document from the Employees collection, with their properties displayed in cells. By clicking on a Display button, as visible in Figure 3-4, you can show or hide specific properties.

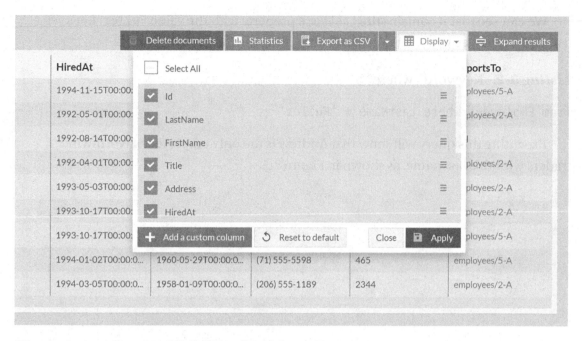

Figure 3-4. *Adjusting Visibility of Employee Properties*

The initial configuration of visible properties will show you only some of them. If you would like to preview the whole document, there is a Preview icon in the first column of the table. Click on it, and you will get a complete JSON preview for a specific document.

Filtering

In the previous section, we learned *from*, first, and essential RQL keyword. It will be a part of every RQL query you make. We saw it used with a collection name, `from Employees`, to return all nine Employee documents.

However, this is a trivial example exercised on sample data. In real-life applications, you will rarely have unbounded queries of this kind. Imagine a company with 10,000 employees – not only that it would take a long time to fetch all of them, but you would be able to show just a few of them listed on a screen. What we usually want to do in applications is fetching and showing a specific subset of collection documents. Looking again at the structure of an Employee with an id `employees/2-A`

```
{
    "LastName": "Fuller",
    "FirstName": "Andrew",
    ...
```

73

We can see that it contains the `LastName` property with the value `Fuller`. Let's see a list of all employee with that same last name using the query in Listing 3-2.

Listing 3-2. Keyword "where"

```
from Employees where LastName = 'Fuller'
```

Executing this query will show that Andrew is the only employee of Northwind traders with this last name, as shown in Figure 3-5.

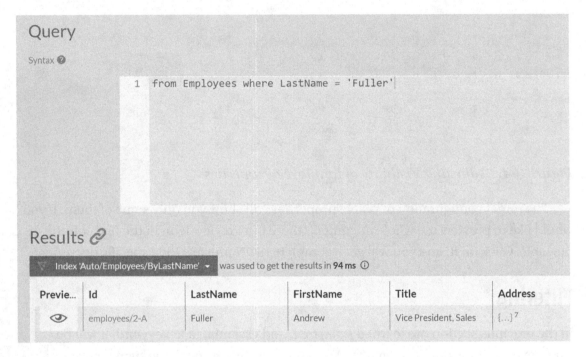

Figure 3-5. *Filtering Employees by the Value of LastName Property*

Compared with a Listing 3-1, we took `from Employees` and added `where LastName = 'Fuller'`. Keyword `where` is used for filtering, i.e., selecting all documents by a certain condition. In this case, the filtering condition is expressed in the form `[propertyName]= '[value]'`. Following this pattern, we can fetch all employees with the first name Andrew using the query in Listing 3-3.

Listing 3-3. Filtering all Employees with the first name Andrew

```
from Employees where FirstName = 'Andrew'
```

Executing this query will produce the same result of just one document – Andrew Fuller has a unique first and last name on the company level.

In our examples, the string value that we use for filtering is surrounded by apostrophes, but we can use quotation marks as well:

```
from Employees where FirstName = "Andrew"
```

which will produce the same result.

Query by Nonexistent Property

What happens if we attempt to filter by nonexistent property, as in Listing 3-4?

Listing 3-4. Filtering all Employees by absent property

```
from Employees where FistName = 'Andrew'
```

In Listing 3-4, we made an intentional typo – `FistName`. If you are a developer accustomed to relational databases, you will expect to receive an error upon executing this query.

However, in RavenDB, an attempt to filter a collection by the nonexistent property name will not produce any errors. You will get an empty result set. Why is that? If you recall, RavenDB is a schemaless database. In relational databases, a schema is a set of mandatory fields for each table. The schemaless nature of RavenDB collections means the absence of any compulsory structure imposed upon documents belonging to the same collection. There is no such thing as a set of mandatory properties such documents must have. Hence, filtering by any property name you can think of will not produce an error – it may only make an unexpected empty result set.

Query by Non-string Properties

Besides filtering by string values, you can also filter by the property containing a numerical value:

```
from Orders where Freight = 8.53
```

or by the property that holds a Boolean value

```
from Products where Discontinued = true
```

Filtering by Complex Properties

In the previous section, we filtered documents by the value of various properties. All these properties were simple ones, located at the first level of the document. Coming back to the Employee document, shown in Listing 3-5, and looking at the Address property.

Listing 3-5. Structure of Employee JSON Document

```
{
    "LastName": "Fuller",
    "FirstName": "Andrew",
    "Title": "Vice President, Sales",
    "Address": {
        "Line1": "908 W. Capital Way",
        "Line2": null,
        "City": "Tacoma",
        "Region": "WA",
        "PostalCode": "98401",
        "Country": "USA",
        "Location": {
            "Latitude": 47.614329,
            "Longitude": -122.3251939
        }
    },
```

We can see it is complex, consisting of nested properties on several levels. RavenDB enables querying over such properties as well, like in Listing 3-6.

Listing 3-6. Filtering all Employees by nested property

```
from Employees where Address.Country = 'USA'
```

Query from Listing 3-6 will select all employees living in the United States. Pay attention to the format of the property name `Address.Country` – looking at the JSON from Listing 3-5, you will observe that `Country` is a nested property within `Address` property.

Transforming the nested structure of JSON properties into a linear form suitable for filtering queries is straightforward. You will write parent property on the first level (in this case, `Address`), and then add desired property from the second level (in this case, `Country`), separated by a dot.

The same approach is applied with properties on deeper levels. Hence, to filter by `Latitiude` property visible in Listing 3-5, we will first state top-level ancestor `Address` and then descend over `Location` to the `Latitude`. Every time we go one level deeper, we will add a dot as a separator between property names. Hence, our final flattened form is `Address.Location.Latitude`. When reading this concatenated property from left to right, you descend one level every time you run into a dot.

Finally, our filtering query accessing the property on a third level looks like this:

```
from Employees where Address.Location.Latitude = 47.614329
```

and will return all employees living along specified `Latitude`.

Filtering by Id

Following the convention for querying the property name, we might think that filtering by identifier follows the same pattern. However, an attempt to execute

```
from Employees where id = 'employees/2-A'
```

will return an empty result set, even though we can inspect that employee with id `employees/2-A` exists.

Why is this the case? As we saw in the previous chapter, an *identifier* is a unique property called `@id` located within `@metadata`. However, this is a default location of an identifier which is also configurable. Because of this, you need to use function id() that will return the name of the property holding the document identifier.

Aware of this, we can rewrite the previous query as

```
from Employees where id() = 'employees/2-A'
```

and results will show this is our old friend, Andrew Fuller.

Cross-Collection Query

In Listing 3-3, we demonstrated how to query all Employees by their first name. It is also possible to query all documents that contain a specific property with a specified value. RavenDb offers @all_docs keyword, which denotes all documents in all collections within your database. Hence

```
from @all_docs where FirstName = 'Andrew'
```

will find all documents across all collections with a FirstName property containing value Andrew. This query result is the same as Listing 3-3, where we specified the collection name. The reason for this is apparent – only Employee documents have FirstName property.

However, if we query by a property that is present in various collections

```
from @all_docs where Address.Country = 'USA'
```

we will get a result set consisting of documents from various collections, as can be seen in Figure 3-6.

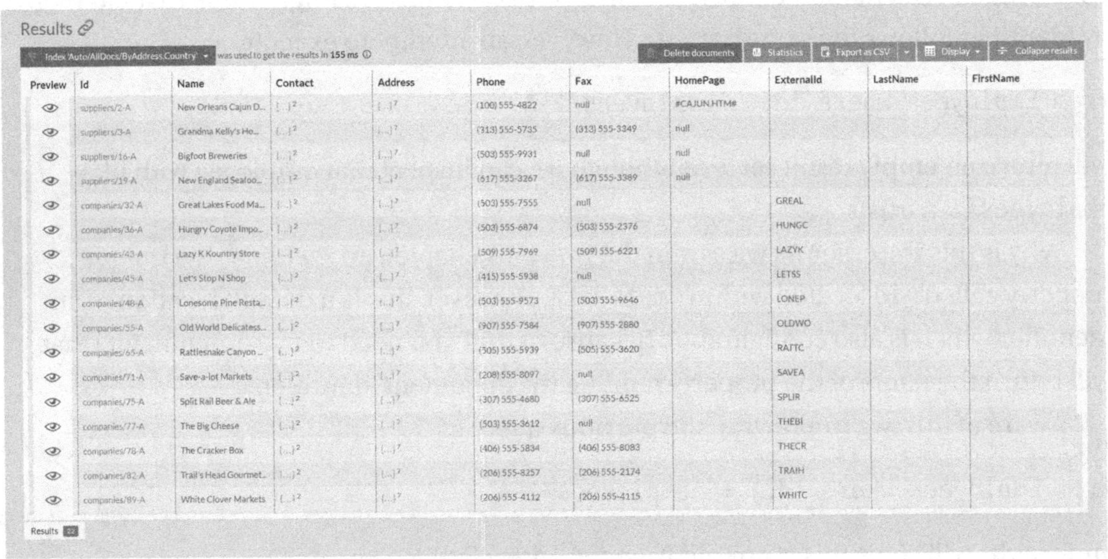

Figure 3-6. *Result of a Query Across All Collections*

This query returned 22 documents in total from Suppliers, Companies, and Employees collection. All these documents represent business entities located in the United States.

It is also possible to write a query that will check which documents from all collections or specific one contain a particular property. Following a query

```
from @all_docs where exists(Address.Country)
```

will return a total of 129 documents that contain `Country` property within `Address` property. However, pay attention that this will also return those documents containing a `null` value for a specific property. From the perspective of RavenDB, nothing is distinguishing `null` – it is a regular value property can have. Hence, `exists()` will check the presence of a specified property, ignoring its content.

Inequality Query

With inequality operator `!=` we can express filtering condition that is the opposite of equality operator `=` usage. For example, executing query

```
from Employees where FirstName != 'Andrew'
```

will select all Employees where the first name is not Andrew.

There is one more way to write this query; you can use `<>` operator, which is a synonym for `!=` operator:

```
from Employees where FirstName <> 'Andrew'
```

Logical Operators

Logical operators are returning Boolean values `true` and `false`. Recalling query from Listing 3-6

```
from Employees where Address.Country = 'USA'
```

we were able to select all employees living in the United States. But what if we want to get all employees living in the United States and United Kingdom? For that purpose, we can use `or` operator:

```
from Employees where Address.Country = 'USA'
or Address.Country = 'UK'
```

Executing this query will result in a union - joint list of employees from one and the other country. However, looking at the previous query, it is obvious that adding additional countries would require lots of typing to produce a chain of conditions. For those cases, we can use IN operator to achieve the same results with a shorter query:

```
from Employees where Address.Country IN ('USA', 'UK')
```

IN operator accepts a list of values and will return true if the stated property has any of the values from the list.

Similar to or operator, and will filter out documents satisfying all stated conditions:

```
from Products where PricePerUnit = 14 and UnitsInStock = 16
```

This query will return two products, products/34-A and products/67-A, which have 16 units in stock and cost 14 per unit.

Following the logic behind or/IN pair, it is logical to ask – is there anything similar to IN, but for and operator. Looking more closely for the applicable case, we would take query like this:

```
from Companies where Address.City = 'London' and Address.City = 'New York'
```

and shorten it. However, a query like this will always return an empty result set – you cannot have a property with two values at once. And, indeed, the single value of a simple property cannot, but complex property that contains multiple values can.

Figure 3-7 shows regions/1-A document with a Territories property which is a collection of territories.

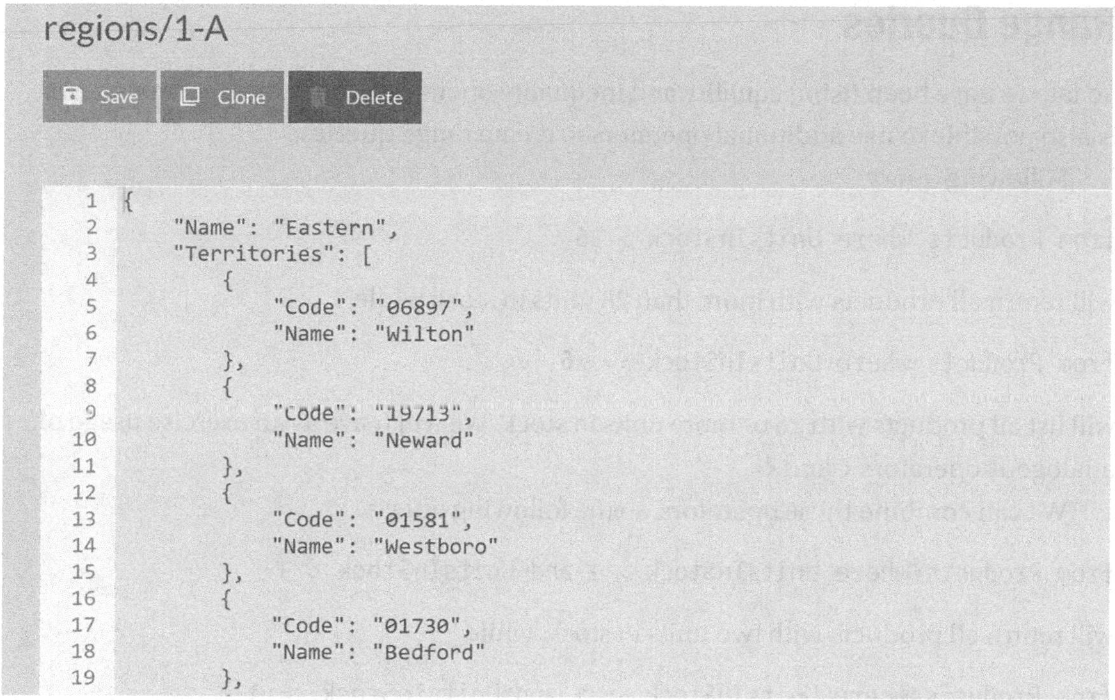

```
regions/1-A

  Save     Clone      Delete


   1  {
   2      "Name": "Eastern",
   3      "Territories": [
   4          {
   5              "Code": "06897",
   6              "Name": "Wilton"
   7          },
   8          {
   9              "Code": "19713",
  10              "Name": "Neward"
  11          },
  12          {
  13              "Code": "01581",
  14              "Name": "Westboro"
  15          },
  16          {
  17              "Code": "01730",
  18              "Name": "Bedford"
  19          },
```

Figure 3-7. *Region Document*

With Territories property, we can now formulate a query that contains and condition

```
from Regions where Territories[].Name = 'Wilton' and Territories[].Name =
'Neward'.
```

This query will return all Regions that have both Wilton and Neward in Territories property. We can shorten it to

```
from Regions where Territories[].Name ALL IN ('Wilton', 'Neward').
```

We can observe two interesting features here. The first one is ALL IN operator that provides a way to match multiple values against an array. The second one is the expression Territories[].Name which is taking all elements of Territories collection and extracting Name property from every element.

A typical use case of the ALL IN operator is selecting all documents tagged with a specified set of tags.

Range Queries

So far, we have been using equality and inequality operator to filter by exact matches. It is also possible to use additional operators to create range queries.

Following query

```
from Products where UnitsInStock > 26
```

will return all products with more than 26 units in stock while

```
from Products where UnitsInStock >= 26
```

will list all products with 26 or more units in stock. We will leave as an exercise usage of analogous operators < and <=.

We can combine these operators, so the following query

```
from Products where UnitsInStock > 1 and UnitsInStock < 3
```

will return all products with two units in stock, while

```
from Products where UnitsInStock >= 1 and UnitsInStock <= 3
```

lists all products that have one, two, or three units in stock.

We can shorten the last query – in the spirit of IN and ALL IN operators, RavenDB also has BETWEEN operator so that we can rewrite the previous query to

```
from Products where UnitsInStock BETWEEN 1 and 3
```

Note that BETWEEN is inclusive on the lower and higher end of an interval.

Casing

Revisiting our familiar example from Listing 3-3, we can modify it like this:

```
from Employees where FirstName = 'ANDREW'
```

Even though you might expect no results, since we capitalized all letters in the name, this query will return Andrew Fuller as the only result. Why is that?

RavenDB defaults to case-insensitive matching in queries. In this case, the value of the filtering condition was different from the actual property in the document, but *Andrew* and *ANDREW* matched since RavenDB ignores casing differences. This case insensitivity was a conscious decision since, in most scenarios, case-insensitive comparison of strings will produce results as you desire.

However, in some specific cases, like matching BASE64 encoded strings, you need exact matching. RavenDB supports that via the `exact()` method, and the following query will return an empty list of results:

```
from Employees where exact(FirstName = 'ANDREW')
```

Full-Text Searching

The ability to perform a full-text search over data is one of the standard features in modern applications. This kind of search will inevitably be present in most of the applications you will be building over time. Fortunately, this is one of the areas where RavenDB excels. We will provide more information in chapters to come, but for now, let's just say that RavenDB uses Lucene.net internally for indexing purposes. Lucene is one of the best indexing engines available today, and over the years, it has established itself as a reliable and standard solution. As a part of an infrastructure, it has been present in several brand-name products, like Solr and Elastic Search. So, RavenDB can provide you with first-class full-text searching capabilities and eliminate a need for any additional solution that would provide you with this.

An example of this type of search would be querying all employees for a common prefix of their first name:

```
from Employees where StartsWith(FirstName, 'an')
```

This query uses the `StartsWith()` function that will match the content of the `FirstName` property of every employee with the prefix *an*. After executing it, you will get results, as shown in Figure 3-8.

Preview	Id	LastName	FirstName	Title	Address	HiredAt
👁	employees/9-A	Dodsworth	Anne	Sales Representative	{...}⁷	1994-11-15T00:
👁	employees/2-A	Fuller	Andrew	Vice President, Sales	{...}⁷	1992-08-14T00:

Figure 3-8. Searching Employees by the Prefix of FirstName

We got two results, two employees, both having first names that start with "an." Note that in this case, we have a case-insensitive query as well.

Besides searching by prefix, it is also possible to search for a term at any position within a field. For example, if we want to search for all companies that contain word *stop* within the name, we would write the following query:

```
from Companies where Search(Name, 'stop')
```

When executed, this query will return two companies, "Let's Stop N Shop" and "QUICK-Stop" as shown in Figure 3-9.

Results 🔗

Index 'Auto/Companies/BySearch(Name)' ▾ was used to get the results in **97 ms** ⓘ

Preview	Id	Name	ExternalId	Contact
👁	companies/45-A	Let's Stop N Shop	LETSS	{...}²
👁	companies/63-A	QUICK-Stop	QUICK	{...}²

Figure 3-9. *Searching Companies by the Name Content*

Both of these companies contain the word "stop" as a part of their name.

It is clear what happens when we perform equality filtering, where exact matching is done, but what happens behind the scene in this case, where partial matching on the arbitrary position can happen? To provide this functionality, RavenDB will take the Name of the company and apply *tokenization*: the name will be split into words, and every such word will be indexed. As an example, the company name "Let's Stop N Shop" would be divided into four tokens: "Let", "Stop", "N", "Shop". After you execute a full-text search query, RavenDB will match your search term against a set of tokens and show you results. So, you could say that full-text search is still exact matching, but not against full property value – instead, components (tokens) are matched.

We can also search by more than one term. Following query

```
from Companies where Search(Name, "monde cheese")
```

will search for all companies that contain "monde" or "cheese" in their name, returning three companies as a result set, as shown in Figure 3-10.

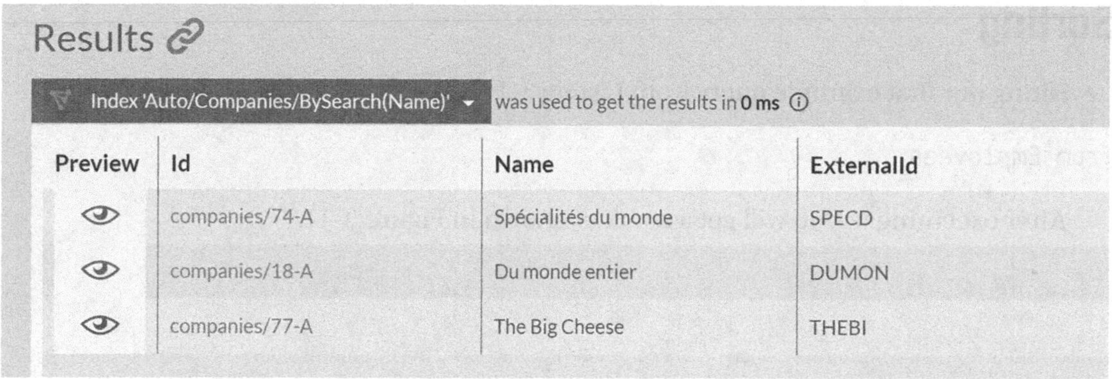

Figure 3-10. *Searching Companies by the Name Content with Multiple Terms*

What about properties which are not simple, but complex instead? Address is a familiar example of such nested property

```
"Address": {
    "Line1": "87 Polk St. Suite 5",
    "Line2": null,
    "City": "San Francisco",
    "Region": "CA",
    "PostalCode": "94117",
    "Country": "USA",
    "Location": {
        "Latitude": 37.7774357,
        "Longitude": -122.4180503
    }
}
```

RavenDB will apply a tokenization process with nested properties as well; first, it will separate complex property into a set of nested properties. After that, every nested property will be tokenized – separated into simple components – and indexed. As a result, when you execute a query

```
from Companies where Search(Address, "London Sweden")
```

you will get a list of companies located in London or Sweden. As you can see, all properties of the Address are indexed, so the full-text search is simultaneously checking both City and Country fields.

Sorting

Revisiting our first example query from Listing 3-1

```
from Employees
```

After executing it, you will get a result as shown in Figure 3-11.

Results 🔗

📄 **Employees** collection was used to get the results in **0 ms** ⓘ

Preview	Id	LastName	FirstName	Title	Address	HiredAt
👁	employees/9-A	Dodsworth	Anne	Sales Representative	[...]⁷	1994-11-15T0(
👁	employees/1-A	Davolio	Nancy	Sales Representative	[...]⁷	1992-05-01T0(
👁	employees/2-A	Fuller	Andrew	Vice President, Sales	[...]⁷	1992-08-14T0(
👁	employees/3-A	Leverling	Janet	Sales Representative	[...]⁷	1992-04-01T0(
👁	employees/4-A	Peacock	Margaret	Sales Representative	[...]⁷	1993-05-03T0(
👁	employees/5-A	Buchanan	Steven	Sales Manager	[...]⁷	1993-10-17T0(
👁	employees/6-A	Suyama	Michael	Sales Representative	[...]⁷	1993-10-17T0(
👁	employees/7-A	King	Robert	Sales Representative	[...]⁷	1994-01-02T0(
👁	employees/8-A	Callahan	Laura	Inside Sales Coordina...	[...]⁷	1994-03-05T0(

Results 9

Figure 3-11. *Unsorted Listing of All Employees*

As you can see, we got all employees, but their order is arbitrary; they are unsorted. RavenDB provides order by clause for sorting results; hence

```
from Employees order by LastName asc
```

will sort employees by the last name in ascending order. You can also specify more than one field for sorting, so

```
from Employees order by LastName asc, FirstName asc
```

will apply secondary sorting by the first name in all those cases when two employees have the same last name.

Sorting is also possible on numeric fields:

```
from Products order by PricePerUnit desc
```

Executing this query results in sorted products, as shown in Figure 3-12.

Results 🔗

Preview	Id	Name	Supplier	Category	QuantityPerUnit	PricePerUnit
👁	products/9-A	Mishi Kobe Niku	suppliers/4-A	categories/6-A	18 - 500 g pkgs.	97
👁	products/41-A	Jack's New England ...	suppliers/19-A	categories/8-A	12 - 12 oz cans	9.65
👁	products/45-A	Rogede sild	suppliers/21-A	categories/8-A	1k pkg.	9.5
👁	products/47-A	Zaanse koeken	suppliers/22-A	categories/3-A	10 - 4 oz boxes	9.5
👁	products/19-A	Teatime Chocolate Bi...	suppliers/8-A	categories/3-A	10 boxes x 12 pieces	9.2
👁	products/23-A	Tunnbröd	suppliers/9-A	categories/5-A	12 - 250 g pkgs.	9
👁	products/20-A	Sir Rodney's Marmal...	suppliers/8-A	categories/3-A	30 gift boxes	81
👁	products/75-A	Rhönbräu Klosterbier	suppliers/12-A	categories/1-A	24 - 0.5 l bottles	7.75
👁	products/54-A	Tourtière	suppliers/25-A	categories/6-A	16 pies	7.45

Index 'Auto/Products/ByPricePerUnitAndUnitsInStockAndUnitsOnOrder' ▾   was used to get the results in **0 ms** ⓘ

Results **77**

Figure 3-12. *Sorted Listing of All Products*

However, looking closely at the column PricePerUnit reveals it is not sorted in the descending order as we expect. Why is this happening, and how to correctly sort Products by this column?

The cause of this lies in the way that RavenDB treats stored data. Fields are not typed, and without us expressing intention, RavenDB will default to lexical ordering, i.e., fields are treated as strings by default. With descending lexical ordering, 81 will come before 9, and that explains the sorting order we got.

Luckily, we can quickly fix this. We need to tell RavenDB which sorting order to apply:

```
from Products order by PricePerUnit as double desc
```

This query will use ordering by treating the field as values of type *double*. We can also apply as `long` to truncate any decimal parts and to compare such truncated values as integers

```
from Products order by PricePerUnit as long desc.
```

Paging

Paging is a common feature in most business applications. Every time you need to show results listing that is longer than the size of the screen, you will most likely use paging. RavenDB natively supports paging with a syntax that looks like this:

```
from Companies limit 10, 5
```

This query will skip the first ten results and return the next five. Of course, paging can be combined with other features, so query

```
from Companies where Address.Country = 'USA' order by Name asc limit 5, 5
```

will filter companies from the United States, order them by name in ascending order, skip the first five, and take the next five.

Advanced Querying

In the previous section, we saw an introduction to RQL and basic filtering, ordering, and paging operations. Now we will look into advanced functions – projections, aggregations, and includes.

Projecting Results

So far, all of our queries were returning complete documents. For example

```
from Employees order by LastName asc
```

will sort employees by the last name and return all of them as full documents. However, when building applications, you will rarely need whole documents. You will usually display a subset of document fields. For example, we might want to show just the first and last name of each employee. RavenDB has a dedicated keyword select that is used precisely for this purpose and works similarly to SQL equivalent, as shown in Listing 3-7.

Listing 3-7. Usage of select keyword

```
from Employees order by LastName asc
select FirstName, LastName
```

Executing this query will produce results as shown in Figure 3-13.

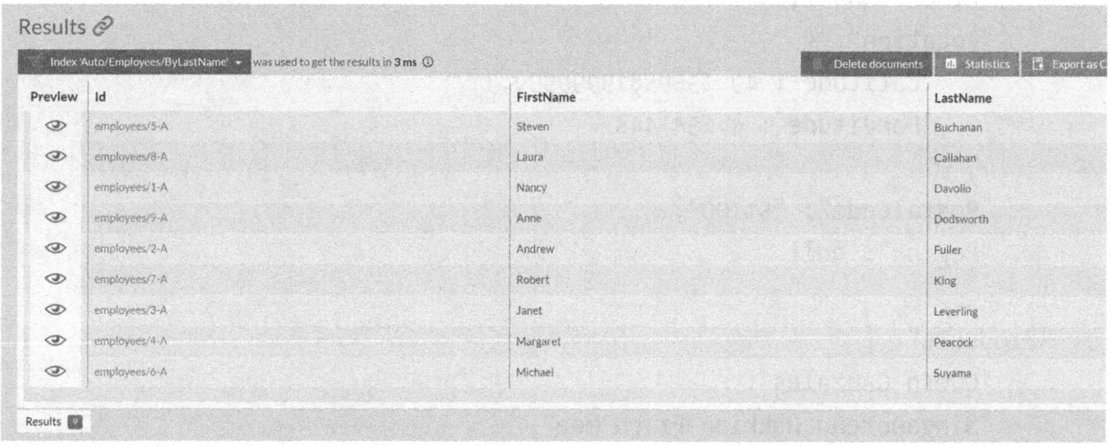

Figure 3-13. *Results of Using Select Keyword*

As you can see, `select` is very similar to the SQL variant – it will select and return only a subset of fields.

You can rename returned fields by using aliases with select statements. Hence, query

```
from Employees
select FirstName as Name, Address.City as City
```

will return a list of documents with the following structure:

```
{
    "Name": "Andrew",
    "City": "Tacoma",
}
```

Projections can also operate on values that are not simple. In the following example, we are using projection on the object and an array:

```
from Orders
select ShipTo, Lines[].ProductName as Products
```

Executing this query will return documents with the following structure:

```
{
    "ShipTo": {
        "City": "Reims",
        "Country": "France",
```

```
        "Line1": "59 rue de l'Abbaye",
        "Line2": null,
        "Location": {
            "Latitude": 49.25595819999999,
            "Longitude": 4.1547448
        },
        "PostalCode": "51100",
        "Region": null
    },
    "Products": [
        "Queso Cabrales",
        "Singaporean Hokkien Fried Mee",
        "Mozzarella di Giovanni"
    ]
}
```

ShipTo object is selected as it is, and Products property contains projection composed of product name selected from all order lines.

Projecting with Object Literals

The projections we saw so far were simple, flat, and linear. They essentially mimicked SQL projections, where you would select a subset of properties to return as a simple collection of linear values. RQL can do much more – you can project a complex result using *object literal* syntax, like in Listing 3-8.

Listing 3-8. Projecting with object literal

```
from Orders as o
select {
    Country: o.ShipTo.Country,
    FirstProduct: o.Lines[0].ProductName,
    LastProduct:  o.Lines[o.Lines.length - 1].ProductName
}
```

When executed, this query returns a set of projections. For document `orders/1-A`, it looks like this:

```
{
    "Country": "France",
    "FirstProduct": "Queso Cabrales",
    "LastProduct": "Mozzarella di Giovanni",
    "@metadata": {
            "@id": "orders/1-A"
    }
}
```

As you can see, we used a simple path to select shipping country and complex expressions to perform a deep selection of first and last product from order lines collection. Notice that in Listing 3-8, we had to use an alias `as  o` to be able to reference `o` in complex projection expressions.

What is also essential about Listing 3-8 is that object literal is not JSON expression – it is JavaScript literal, and any valid JavaScript expression will be executed. As an example of this, we can look into the `HiredAt` property of an Employee document:

```
"HiredAt": "1994-03-05T00:00:00.0000000"
```

This string represents a date in ISO 8601 format, and with object literal, it is possible to write JavaScript, like one in Listing 3-9, that will process this date and extract the year.

Listing 3-9. Projecting with JavaScript within object literal

```
from Employees as e
select {
    Id: id(e),
    Year: new Date(e.HiredAt).getFullYear(),
    Fullname: e.FirstName + " " + e.LastName
}
```

will return a set of documents with the following structure:

```
{
    "Id": "employees/9-A",
    "Year": 1994,
    "Fullname": "Anne Dodsworth"
}
```

Query in Listing 3-9 is using JavaScript to populate all three fields:

- Id – calling function id() that is taking document as an argument and determines its identifier.

- Year – calling JS constructor for Date object with ISO 8601 string as an argument. After that, method Date.getFullYear() returns year.

- Fullname – concatenates two properties of the document with a separator.

Declaring Functions in Queries

With RQL, you can extract JavaScript code into functions that you can call from object literals, as we did in Listing 3-10.

Listing 3-10. Calling JavaScript function from object literal

```
declare function getFullName(e)
{
    return e.FirstName + " " + e.LastName;
}

from Employees as e
select {
    Id: id(e),
    Year: new Date(e.HiredAt).getFullYear(),
    Fullname: getFullName(e)
}
```

In this example, we extracted code that was joining first and last name into function getFullname(), which is then called from object literal.

You can have several of these functions. Their limitations are standard limitations of JavaScript with additional constraints from the nature of their usage. If JavaScript code takes 5 seconds to execute, your query will be additionally 5 seconds longer. Taking all of this into account, you can produce arbitrary complex functionality, demonstrated in an example from Listing 3-11.

Listing 3-11. Example of complex JavaScript code in object literal

```
declare function lineItemPrice(l) {
    return l.PricePerUnit * l.Quantity * (1 - l.Discount);
}

from Orders as o
select {
    TopProducts: o.Lines
        .sort((a, b) => lineItemPrice(b) - lineItemPrice(a) )
        .map(x => x.ProductName)
        .slice(0,2),
    Total: o.Lines.reduce((acc, l) => acc + lineItemPrice(l), 0)
}
```

When executed, code from Listing 3-11 will produce a list of documents with a total value of the order and two most expensive products from each order, e.g.

```
{
    "TopProducts": [
        "Mozzarella di Giovanni",
        "Queso Cabrales"
    ],
    "Total": 440
}
```

Aggregation

Aggregation is the process of grouping data. In this section, we will examine how RQL can provide data aggregations and enable you to sum up your documents in various ways.

If you recall, every order has Company property that contains the Id of the company, as shown in Figure 3-14.

	Id	Company	Employee	Freight	OrderedAt
☐	orders/830-A	companies/65-A	employees/1-A	8.53	1998-05-06T00:00:...
☐	orders/829-A	companies/9-A	employees/4-A	38.28	1998-05-06T00:00:...
☐	orders/828-A	companies/68-A	employees/8-A	6.19	1998-05-06T00:00:...
☐	orders/827-A	companies/73-A	employees/7-A	18.44	1998-05-06T00:00:...
☐	orders/826-A	companies/58-A	employees/2-A	24.95	1998-05-05T00:00:...
☐	orders/825-A	companies/20-A	employees/4-A	258.64	1998-05-05T00:00:...
☐	orders/824-A	companies/46-A	employees/1-A	0.93	1998-05-05T00:00:...
☐	orders/823-A	companies/44-A	employees/2-A	136	1998-05-05T00:00:...
☐	orders/822-A	companies/80-A	employees/1-A	15.67	1998-05-04T00:00:...
☐	orders/821-A	companies/62-A	employees/8-A	81.75	1998-05-04T00:00:...

Figure 3-14. *Orders have Company Property with Company Identifier*

Let's find the number of the orders every company has in our database, shown in Listing 3-12.

Listing 3-12. Grouping orders by companies

```
from Orders
group by Company
select Company, count()
```

As you might have expected, an appropriate keyword for this is group indeed. After executing this query, we will get results as shown in Figure 3-15.

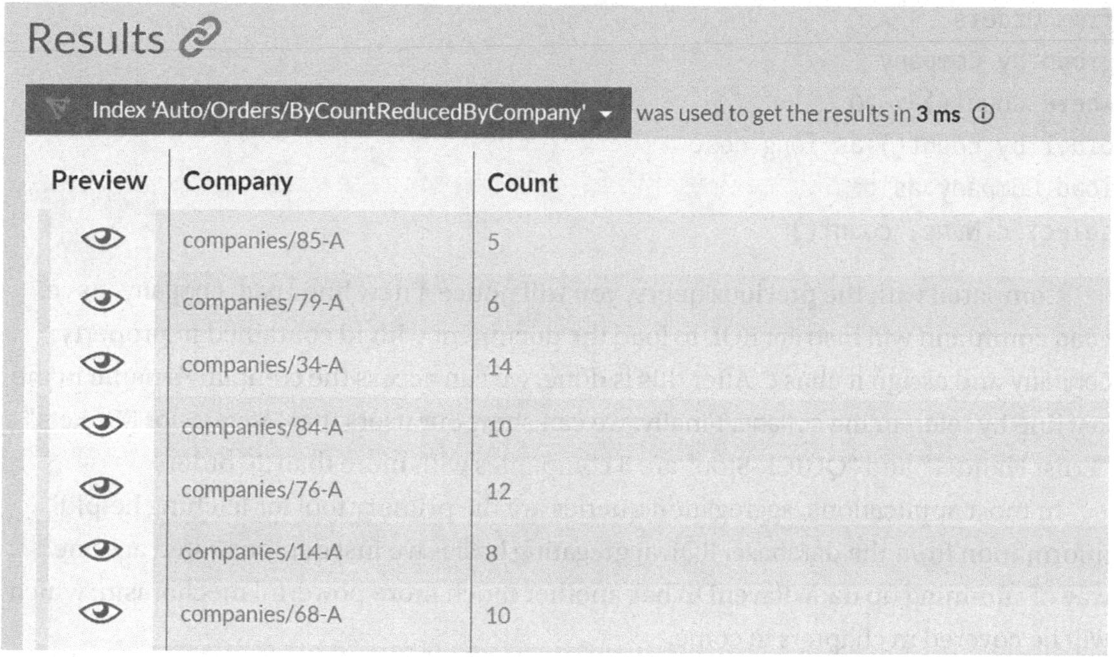

Results 🔗

Index 'Auto/Orders/ByCountReducedByCompany' ▾   was used to get the results in **3 ms** ⓘ

Preview	Company	Count
👁	companies/85-A	5
👁	companies/79-A	6
👁	companies/34-A	14
👁	companies/84-A	10
👁	companies/76-A	12
👁	companies/14-A	8
👁	companies/68-A	10

Figure 3-15. *Orders Grouped by the Company*

The next step in our analysis would be sorting this list in descending order:

```
from Orders
group by Company
order by count() as long desc
select Company, count()
```

and after that, filtering only those with more than 20 orders

```
from Orders
group by Company
where count() > 20
order by count() as long desc
select Company, count()
```

We should always think of queries as a way to extract data for displaying on the application screen. From that perspective, it is easy to see that informing users about companies "companies/71-A," "companies/20-A," and "companies/63-A" is not too user-friendly. So, as the last step in this brief analysis, we will replace company identifiers with the actual name of the company:

```
from Orders
group by Company
where count() > 20
order by count() as long desc
load Company as c
select c.Name, count()
```

Compared with the previous query, you will notice a new line load Company as c. Load command will instruct RQL to load the document with id contained in property Company and assign it alias c. After this is done, we can access the company's name in the last line by referencing c.Name. Finally, we can show our users that "Save-a-lot Markets," "Ernst Handel," and "QUICK-Stop" are 3 companies with more than 20 orders.

In most applications, aggregation queries are the primary tool for fetching helpful information from the database. RQL aggregating basics we just demonstrated are one way of summing up data. RavenDB has another much more powerful mechanism, which will be covered in chapters to come.

Handling Relationships

In the previous chapter on Modeling, we learned about suitable and appropriate modeling principles that will result in documents with a balanced level of independency, isolation, and coherency. However, even with such documents, you will still need to combine them into view models that combine properties from two or more documents into a form suitable for visual representation. Let's look at how RavenDB can support you in such scenarios.

Accessing Related Documents

At the end of a previous section, we used Load() to access related documents. In a nontrivial application, your model will consist of aggregates referencing other documents. Let's look at one such document, order with id orders/830-A:

```
{
    "Company": "companies/65-A",
    "Employee": "employees/1-A",
    "Freight": 8.53,
    "Lines": [
    ...
```

Displaying the order in this form to the user does not bring too much value – the user would have to check which company hides behind id companies/65-A manually.

To show this order on the screen with complete information, we would have to make two more calls to the database to load referenced company and employee. To optimize this, RQL provides you with a Load() function that accepts a reference to the document and returns referenced document. This way, instead of three calls to the database, we can perform just one call and fetch complete information about this order, as demonstrated in Listing 3-13.

Listing 3-13. Loading reference Company and Employee

```
from Orders as o
where id() = 'orders/830-A'
load o.Company as c, o.Employee as e
select {
    CompanyName: c.Name,
    EmployeeName: e.FirstName + " " + e.LastName
}
```

When executed, this query will return the following projection:

```
{
    "CompanyName": "Rattlesnake Canyon Grocery",
    "EmployeeName": "Nancy Davolio"
}
```

As you can see in Listing 3-13, we provided load with a list of references and aliases for dereferenced documents. After that, in select projection, we can use documents c and e.

An important thing to notice here is the order of the execution. Going over keywords in Listing 3-13, there is the following order:

- From

- Where

- Load

- Select

RavenDB will take the `from-where` part of the query and run it, producing interim results. After that, RavenDB will execute `load()` to fetch documents referenced from interim results. Finally, select will create a projection that is the final result set of this query. It is essential to note the order here – load is applied in the end, after results have been filtered and fetched and basic query execution completes. Because of this, `load()` does not impact the cost of the query.

If you compare this with relational databases, you will see that the order of execution is significantly different. You would write a query that would first perform *join* that would provide access to referenced rows and then apply filtering on joined tables. However, please pay attention that we would join all rows from these tables and then perform filtering. In other words, the RDBMS engine would spend cycles joining rows, only to discard them after filtering is applied. RavenDB optimizes not only on this but also on many other things. As a result, your applications will be faster, and the amount of work for the same queries will be lower.

You can also use `load()` directly in projections or in JavaScript functions, as can be seen in the following example:

```
declare function getFullName(empId)
{
    var e = load(empId);
    return e.FirstName + " " + e.LastName;
}

from Orders as o
where id() = 'orders/830-A'
select {
    CompanyName: load(o.Company).Name,
    EmployeeName: getFullName(o.Employee)
}
```

Include

Besides using projections, there is one more way to access related documents. RQL provides `include`, which is another way to reduce the number of round trips you need to make to fetch complete information:

```
from Orders
where id() = 'orders/830-A'
include Company, Employee
```

This query will return a complete order document, but also, in the same round trip to the database, it will produce two additional collections, as shown in Figure 3-16.

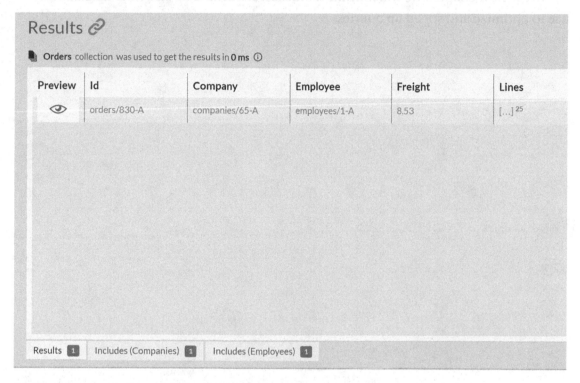

Figure 3-16. Order with Included Company and Employee

At the bottom of Figure 3-16, you can see two more result sets. Since we have just one order returned, these two collections contain just one company and just one employee.

Include syntax is intended to be used when you want to fetch the complete document from the database and pull along all related documents in the same round trip to the database. You will then perform some additional operations on these documents without being forced to make any more requests to the database.

Summary

In this chapter, we covered writing queries in RavenDB. Besides filtering, querying, and paging, we also covered advanced topics - projections, aggregations, and dereferencing relations.

In the next chapter, we will introduce indexes, a crucial data structure all databases use to optimize and speed up queries.

CHAPTER 4

Indexes

In the previous chapter, we saw how to run queries that will return data that you need. This chapter will cover what happens behind the scenes when you run such queries and how the database executes them. We will also show some challenges database needs to solve and how databases are coping with ever-growing data. This chapter will present some possible optimization solutions. Finally, we will show how RavenDB prevents common problems with queries.

Queries from the Perspective of a Database

As users and developers, we execute queries against the database to get results back. This action is so standard that we do not think about underlying mechanisms and tools that deliver results. Additionally, working with a relational database, you probably use Object-Relational Mapper, representing an additional layer of abstraction between your code and a database. Over time, as we work with databases, we tend to forget what happens behind the scene.

Unbounded Queries

The first important notion is the concept of the *unbounded query*. Such queries will return whole collections without any limitations. When executed, they will return all documents from a collection, no matter how many you have. Even if you have one million employees, you will get them all back. Listing 4-1 shows a simple unbounded query.

Listing 4-1. Unbounded query over Employees collection

```
from Employees
```

© Dejan Miličić 2022
D. Miličić, *Introducing RavenDB*, https://doi.org/10.1007/978-1-4842-8919-8_4

The database engine will fetch all employees from the disk and return them. Unbounded queries can be dangerous, as things are not under your control. Results of execution are not deterministic, but they depend on the number of documents. If we are processing employees, we do not know if we will iterate over 10 or 10,000 employees. Furthermore, for all visual representations of our company employees, we will rarely need all of them.

Paging

Usually, we want to present paged list or some variant of paging (e.g., fetching batches as the user scrolls down the list). As shown in the previous chapter, RavenDB has built-in support for paging in the following form:

```
from [Collection] limit [skip], [take]
```

so query `from Employees limit 0, 2` will return first two employees.

However, besides paged result set, it is also possible to get a total number of documents in a collection in the same round trip to the database. As shown in Figure 4-1, there is a *chain icon* next to the *Results* heading.

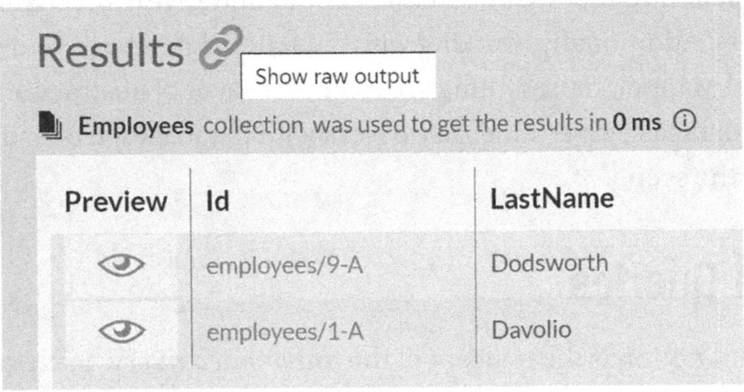

Figure 4-1. *Show Raw Output Icon*

Clicking on this icon will display raw JSON that RavenDB Server returns:

```
{
    TotalResults: 9,
    LongTotalResults: 9,
    CappedMaxResults: 2,
    ...
```

The client interprets this response, in this case, RavenDB Studio, to show you query results. Not all properties of returned JSON are rendered in Studio – as you can see, the first property contains a total number of results. So, you can display the total number of results in paged query with just one request to the server.

Filtering

However, this simple request is what we rarely need – we usually want to filter out employees by a specific field. So, let's see which one of these nine employees in our database live and work in London, as defined in the query in Listing 4-2.

Listing 4-2. The query for employees living in London

```
from Employees
where Address.City = 'London'
```

Figure 4-2 shows the result of executing this query.

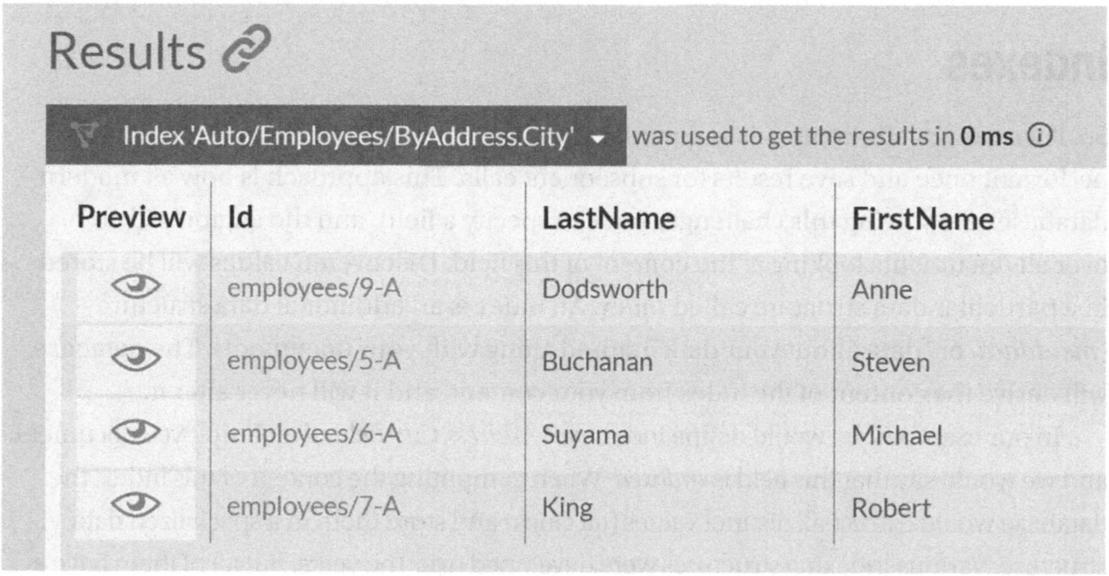

Results 🔗

Index 'Auto/Employees/ByAddress.City' ▼ was used to get the results in **0 ms** ⓘ

Preview	Id	LastName	FirstName
👁	employees/9-A	Dodsworth	Anne
👁	employees/5-A	Buchanan	Steven
👁	employees/6-A	Suyama	Michael
👁	employees/7-A	King	Robert

Figure 4-2. *Employees Living in London*

As you can see, the engine managed to find those living in London. So, if you had to perform the same task, how would you do it?

Let's imagine that you have nine papers representing each of the employees. Taking one by one, you would look at the Address, checking if City is London. If this is the case, you will stack paper to the right. Otherwise, you would put it to the left. After you process all documents, the stack to the right will contain all four employees living in London.

What you just did is very similar to what a database engine might do in some cases, and it is called *sequential scan* or *full table scan*. It might seem like a logical move at first sight. However, what happens as the number of employees grows in your database? Or, if you filter orders in a retail operation, you have thousands and thousands of orders after a couple of years. How long will it take to filter orders by some of their properties? No matter how fast the disk or CPU, your application will start suffering from a full table scan sooner or later.

In algorithmic complexity terms, this operation has O(n) complexity – if you increase the amount of data ten times, filtering will take ten times longer. It is evident that this approach is not a sustainable one and that we need a different one. However, no matter what method we use, the database engine still needs to visit every employee to check the living city.

Indexes

So, if we cannot eliminate this sequential scan, one conceptual solution would be to perform it once and save results for subsequent calls. This approach is how all modern databases are solving this challenge. You can specify a field, and the engine will go over all documents looking at the content of this field. Discovered values will be stored in a particular data structure called *Index*. An index is an additional data structure (*metadata*, or "data about your data") stored along with your documents. The database will derive the content of the index from your content, and it will never alter it.

In our example, we would define index over *Address.City* field of an Employee document, and we would say that this field is *indexed*. When computing the content of this index, the database would extract all distinct values (all cities) and store them in a specialized data structure. Various indexing structures were developed over the years, but all of them have a clear purpose – to provide a fast way to fetch documents based on some criteria.

After forming *Employee.Address.City* index and populating it with all cities where employees live, the database engine will be able to answer our queries swiftly, whatever value may be. When we execute the quest for all London employees, the engine will not go over documents. Instead, it will consult the index. There it will find entries shown in Table 4-1.

Table 4-1. *Content of Employee.Address.City Index*

Address.City	ID
Kirkland	employees/3-A
London	employees/9-A
	employees/5-A
	employees/6-A
	employees/7-A
Redmond	employees/4-A
Seattle	employees/1-A
	employees/8-A
Tacoma	employees/2-A

Obtaining a list of all employees from London is now easy. Their identifiers will be collected, and those documents will be fetched from the disk and delivered. You could say that we prepared ahead of time for all possible *Address.City* queries. We precomputed results and stored them side-by-side with documents. As a result, our queries will be fast. There are no more table scans: no more need to go over documents and load them to check if they should be included in the result set. We have a list of IDs that can be read directly from the disk, with certainty that this is a complete result set.

Types of Indexes

If a computation is inevitable, there is no way to avoid performing it. However, you can do it just once and save results to a disk ahead of query time. Indexes are precomputed answers stored in a specialized data structure that provides a fast way to fetch results.

In Table 4-1, we presented an index that contains document IDs. Such an index is called the *secondary index*.

When a secondary index is used to service a query, one more step is needed before the list of employees is returned to you. The database needs to use IDs obtained from the secondary index to fetch complete employee documents. This operation needs to be efficient, so the database will maintain one more index that tracks the exact storage position of each document based on its identifier. This index is called the *key-value index*, and if you have been working with relational databases, you will recognize a similar internal data structure as the *primary index*.

Overall, a query like Listing 4-2 will require a database to perform two operations. First, taking the value of an indexed property, a *secondary index* will be consulted to obtain a list of identifiers. Second, the *primary index* will be used to fetch employee documents from database storage efficiently.

However, in certain situations, this can be reduced to just one operation. Namely, you can expand the index to contain the whole document instead of just an identifier. Such index is called *clustered index*, and you can see its structure in Table 4-2.

Table 4-2. *Content of Clustered Index*

City	ID	Document
Kirkland	employees/3-A	{id: "employees/3-A", "FirstName": "Janet"..}
London	employees/9-A	{id: "employees/9-A", "FirstName": "Anne"..}
	employees/5-A	{id: "employees/5-A", "FirstName": "Steven"..}
	employees/6-A	{id: "employees/6-A", "FirstName": "Michael"..}
	employees/7-A	{id: "employees/7-A", "FirstName": "Robert"..}
Redmond	employees/4-A	{id: "employees/4-A", "FirstName": "Margaret"..}
Seattle	employees/1-A	{id: "employees/1-A", "FirstName": "Nancy"..}
	employees/8-A	{id: "employees/8-A", "FirstName": "Laura"..}
Tacoma	employees/2-A	{id: "employees/2-A", "FirstName": "Andrew"..}

The database engine can fetch the list of employee documents with just one round trip to the storage with a clustered index. Unfortunately, such an index is expensive storage-wise since it will essentially duplicate all records from the primary data storage into metadata structure. Various relational databases are using different approaches to overcome this challenge. SQL Server allows just one clustered index per table; MySQL is implementing primary index as clustered, with secondary index entries pointing to primary keys.

Midway between nonclustered index (storing only references) and clustered one (storing complete data) is *covering index*, also known as an *index with included columns*. Let's observe the following query:

```
from Employees
where Address.City = 'London'
select FirstName
```

In this case, we are not asking for a complete employee document. We are interested in the first name of employees from London. Names are usually small pieces of data, and we can expand the nonclustered secondary index from Table 4-1 into the form shown in Table 4-3.

Table 4-3. *Content of Covering Index*

Address.City	ID	FirstName
Kirkland	employees/3-A	Janet
London	employees/9-A	Anne
	employees/5-A	Steven
	employees/6-A	Michael
	employees/7-A	Robert
Redmond	employees/4-A	Margaret
Seattle	employees/1-A	Nancy
	employees/8-A	Laura
Tacoma	employees/2-A	Andrew

Covering index is a compromise that enables the database to answer some of the queries using index alone (hence the term *covered*, since such index covers some of the queries) without allocating too much space.

Downsides of Indexing

Indexes sound like a great idea, but there are also downsides. Storing additional data structures on the disk will inevitably take extra space. In our example, we defined the index on just one field of the Employee document. If we wanted to provide users with efficient filtering on other fields like FirstName or LastName, we would have to expand EmployeeIndex with entries for these two fields. Over time, as you define new indexes, expand existing ones with additional fields, and increase the number of documents in your database, the total size of indexes will inevitably grow, allocating more and more space for this metadata.

However, there is another much more challenging task – index maintenance. Every time we update an employee's city of living or any other indexed field, we need to update the Index. Every time we create a new employee in the database, the Index needs to be updated. As a result, each write to a database will be accompanied by additional one or more index update operations. Both of them, writing data and index updates, will be performed together, making your writing operation slower.

This results in an interesting trade-off: we will introduce indexes to speed up queries, but these will slow down writes. We want to have fast queries, but at the same time, we do not want to slow down writes. Hence, we should carefully select which fields should be indexed based on the applications' usage patterns. This trade-off explains why databases are not indexing everything by default – this approach would introduce unnecessary overhead.

Even though querying via indexes (opposed to querying raw data) is what every developer should be doing, a lack of indexes is probably the most common anti-pattern among programmers. There are various contributing factors to this sad fact, but the need for the manual creation of indexes is the most significant one. It is easy to forget about it or make an omission, even when you are informed and aware. Additionally, this mistake is usually well-hidden in a small amount of data. Developers testing an application on a small dataset will not experience the dreadful consequences of a full table scan. Without load testing, a developer will deliver the database without indexes to production.

Eventually, a lack of indexes will result in a significant and annoying slow-up of the application. With the small amount of data in the database, the application will be fast, but over time, as the amount of data grows, performance will start to degrade linearly. This gradual degradation is a severe obstacle to the scaling of your application and will make you go back and fix performance problems, which will cost you both time and money.

RavenDB's Indexing Philosophy

The general philosophy of RavenDB design as a database is not to help you solve problems and challenges but to prevent them. This approach has unique consequences – your database will make bad things impossible, or when you make an omission, RavenDB will react and correct your actions.

As a part of this prevention philosophy, in RavenDB, all queries are always executed via indexes. It is technically impossible for a query to avoid execution via index. This way, the manual omission is not possible, and all filtering queries will be efficient.

So, what happens when we attempt to run a query from Listing 4-2 without defining the index upfront? Will we get an error or warning? Figure 4-3 shows the result of query execution.

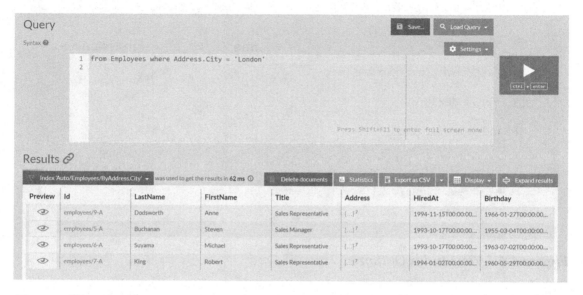

Figure 4-3. *Results Panel*

Not only that an error was not displayed, but we also got the actual result set. How come?

Looking closer at the top left corner of the Results panel, you can see that RavenDB Studio indicates the name of the index used to serve this query. Figure 4-4 shows a close-up of this part of the screen with the index name and execution time.

Figure 4-4. *Index Details*

Index with the name *Auto/Employees/ByAddress.City* was used, and it took 62ms to get results. We can inspect this index by expanding the dropdown and selecting the first option, *View Index*, as shown in Figure 4-5.

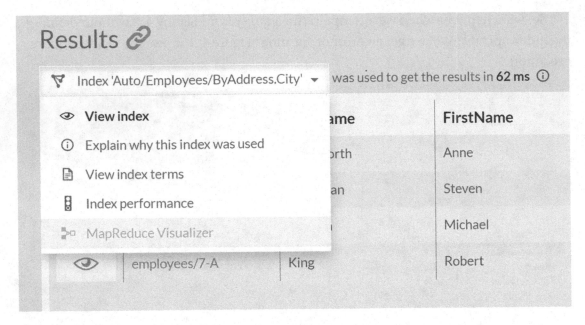

Figure 4-5. *View Index Option*

You can now see mapping structure – documents from Employees collection are processed, and values are extracted from *Address.City* field. Figure 4-6 shows the structure of this index.

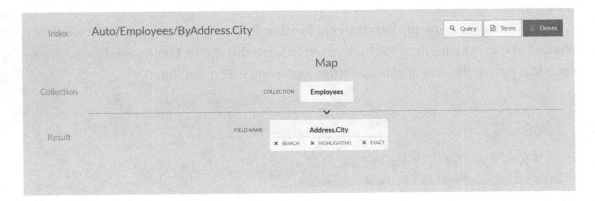

Figure 4-6. *Structure of Index*

RavenDB studio provides a way to inspect the content of this index. If you click on the *Terms* button in the upper right corner, you will be presented with *Index terms*, as shown in Figure 4-7.

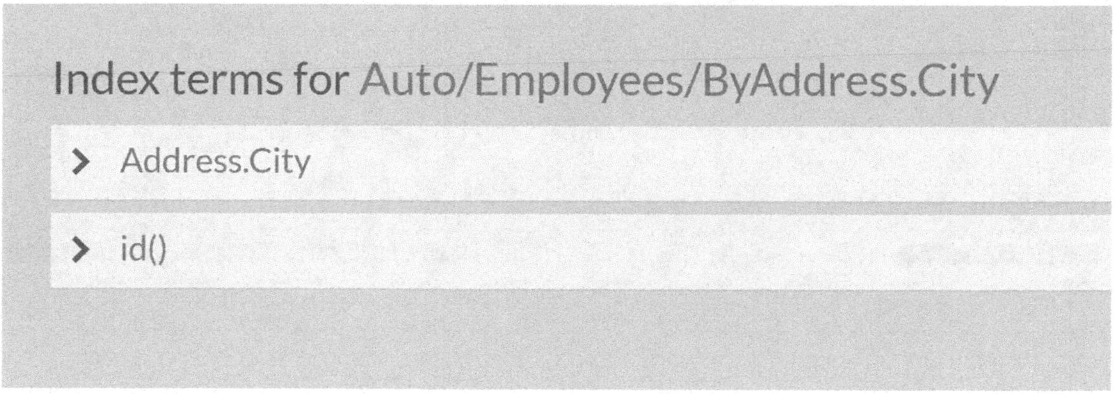

Figure 4-7. *Index Terms*

Expanding both *Address.City* and *id()* sections will reveal extracted values from those fields. It is easy to see that nine employees have unique identifiers (hence we have nine identifiers), but some live in the same city since we have five different cities. We can execute a filtering query against this index by hovering over any of the fields and clicking on magnifying glass icon, as shown in Figure 4-8.

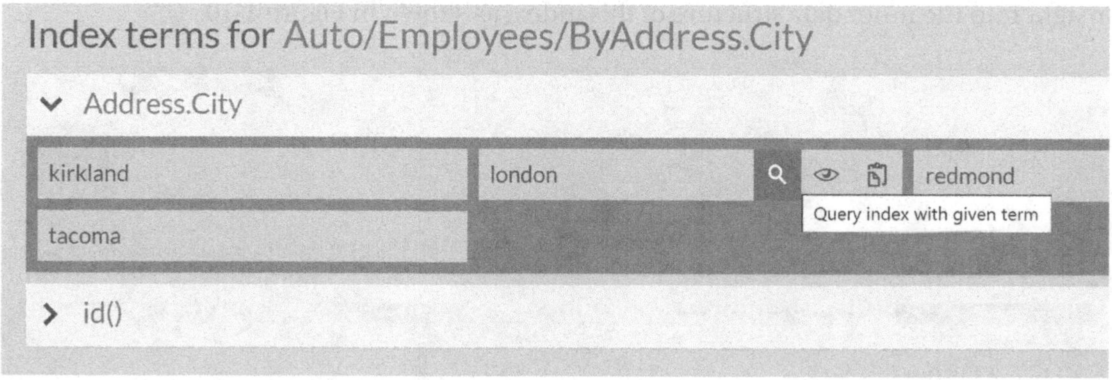

Figure 4-8. *Querying over Index Terms*

Result of executing query

```
from index 'Auto/Employees/ByAddress.City'
where 'Address.City' = 'london'
```

is shown in Figure 4-9.

Figure 4-9. *Results of Executing Query over Index*

As observed in Figure 4-9, we are now querying the index directly, and the results are the same as when we executed the query from Listing 4-2. This is expected since the same index was used when we queried the collection directly.

Studio also provides a way to see the content of this index. Clicking on *Settings* and then turning on *Show the raw index entries instead of matching documents* will produce insight into the inner data structure of this index, as shown in Figure 4-10.

Figure 4-10. *Raw Index Entries*

Looking again at Table 4-1, we can see that this is the precisely same set of entries for "London." Modifying this query and running it for the rest of the cities from Figure 4-8 will return the remaining items from Table 4-1.

Try running `from Employees where Address.City = 'London'` query again. You are getting the expected result set, but what is essential here is the execution time, shown in Figure 4-11.

Figure 4-11. *Query Execution Time*

We did not mention it earlier, but this Query execution time measures server-side execution time. Even if you experienced a long time waiting for results to appear in your browser, you were waiting for the result set to be delivered to your browser. The measurement shown here is the actual time it took the database to generate these results.

Comparing query timing for this attempt with the previous one from Figure 4-3, you can see that we are much faster this time. On the first run, after failing to find an appropriate index, RavenDB had to create one. This operation took some time – the database had to fetch all nine employees from the disk, process their *Address.City* field, extract values, and form an index out of those values.

On the second run that we just did, a suitable index was detected right away and used to deliver results. The same scenario will happen on any subsequent run – precomputed values will be read from the disk and returned.

Summary

In this chapter, we introduced the concept of an index as a specialized data structure. An index is metadata placed side by side with your data inside a database, and it is one of the possible solutions for speeding up queries. We showed how RavenDB's design approach would help you prevent common problems with indexes.

In the next chapter, we will show how you can control index creation and define it yourself instead of letting RavenDB create them automatically.

Map Indexes

The previous chapter introduced the index, which almost all databases use to speed up and optimize queries. In this chapter, we will show how to take control of indexes. Instead of relying on RavenDB to create them automatically, you can specify them explicitly as "static" indexes. Along with ways to index one or multiple collections, you will also learn how to handle referenced documents and create stored, dynamic, and computed fields. Finally, we will cover techniques to index hierarchical data models in your database.

Static Indexes

In the previous chapter, we saw how RavenDB does not allow queries against raw data. Queries are always executed over indexes, and if you do not have one, RavenDB's *query optimizer* will create one for you.

Executing query

```
from Employees where FirstName = 'Nancy'
```

will trigger the creation of the `Auto/Employees/ByFirstName` automatic index. Once created, this index will remain active after the query results are generated, and RavenDB will use it for all future filtering and ordering queries over the same field.

Raven Query Language allows you to query indexes directly, as shown in Listing 5-1

Listing 5-1. Querying index directly

```
from index 'Auto/Employees/ByFirstName' where FirstName = 'Nancy'
```

Such query will produce the same result as a previous query.

Hence, you can either use `from [Collection]` form and let the query optimizer choose for you or go with `from index '[Index_name]'` and take control over the selection of the index used to deliver results.

© Dejan Miličić 2022

D. Miličić, *Introducing RavenDB*, https://doi.org/10.1007/978-1-4842-8919-8_5

You can take control even further. Instead of relying on a query optimizer to create indexes, you can define it yourself. Such indexes are called *static indexes*.

Static Map Index

You can inspect the content of the `Auto/Employees/ByFirstName` automatic index by writing a query:

```
from index 'Auto/Employees/ByFirstName'
```

and then selecting *Settings* ➤ *Show raw index entries instead of matching documents* as visible in Figure 5-1.

Figure 5-1. *Content of Automatic Index*

You can create a static index with the same content from Figure 5-1. Select the *List of Indexes* option in the left column, and then click on the *New index* button. You are now looking at a screen where you can define a new index, shown in Figure 5-2.

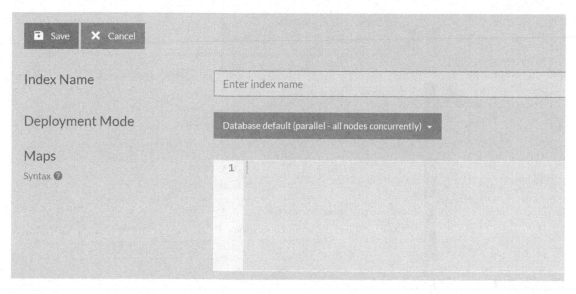

Figure 5-2. *Create a New Index Dialog*

You first need to select a name for the new index. A convention is to go with the names of the form

`[COLLECTION]/By[FIELD]`

and you can already see it with `Auto/Employees/ByFirstName`.

Hence, use `Employees/ByFirstName` for the name.

Content of Map Index is a JavaScript function `map` that will take documents from the collection and return an object for every document; these objects will be index entries. Accordingly, the name `map`, since we are mapping documents to index entries. Listing 5-2 shows such mapping function.

Listing 5-2. Content of `Employees/ByFirstName` index

```
map("Employees", function(emp) {
    return {
        FirstName: emp.FirstName
    }
})
```

Clicking the *Save* button will create a new index, and it will be listed along with other automatic and static ones, as shown in Figure 5-3.

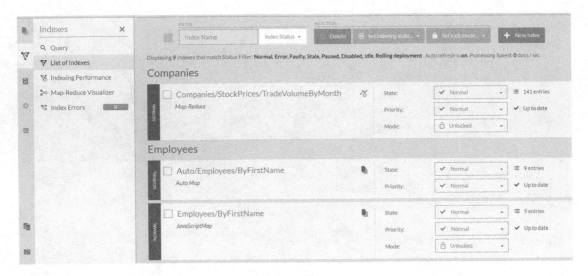

Figure 5-3. *List of Indexes*

You can see that the automatic index `Auto/Employees/ByFirstName` contains nine entries, the same as the `Employees/ByFirstName` you just created. And if you query it

```
from index 'Employees/ByFirstName' where FirstName = 'Nancy'
```

you will get identical results.

Static Index Analysis

Let's analyze all elements of an index from Listing 5-2. Looking at the top-level structure, you can see this map index has the following form:

```
map("[COLLECTION]", function(doc) {...})
```

The first argument is a collection name. One by one, the document will be fetched from that collection and passed to the JavaScript function, which is the second argument.

Looking at the function itself

```
function(emp) {
    return {
        FirstName: emp.FirstName
    }
}
```

CHAPTER 5   MAP INDEXES

you can see it accepts a document from the collection and returns JavaScript *object literal:*

```
{
    FirstName: emp.FirstName
}
```

This object literal will be indexing entry.

Index can be somewhat simplified if we replace traditional function expression with a compact alternative called *arrow function expression* as shown in Listing 5-3.

Listing 5-3. A simplified version of the `Employees/ByFirstName` index

```
map("Employees", emp => {
    return {
        FirstName: emp.FirstName
    }
})
```

Expanding Map Index

The structure of the index entries will limit fields we can filter. Attempting to execute the following query

```
from index 'Employees/ByFirstName' where LastName = 'Davolio'
```

will result in an error:

```
The field 'LastName' is not indexed, cannot query/sort on fields that are
not indexed
```

Your first reaction might be to create new *Employees/ByLastName* index, as shown in Listing 5-4.

Listing 5-4. Employees/ByLastName index

```
map("Employees", emp => {
    return {
        LastName: emp.LastName
    }
})
```

This index now can be queried

```
from index 'Employees/ByLastName' where LastName = 'Davolio'
```

and will produce results.

However, instead of adding one more index, we can expand *Employees/ByFirstName* index with LastName field. Following conventions we previously introduced, we can name it *Employees/ByFirstNameByLastName* and define its content as shown in Listing 5-5.

Listing 5-5. Employees/ByFirstNameByLastName index

```
map("Employees", emp => {
    return {
        FirstName: emp.FirstName,
        LastName: emp.LastName
    }
})
```

Inspecting raw content of this index reveals FirstName and LastName indexed for ID of every document, as visible in Figure 5-4.

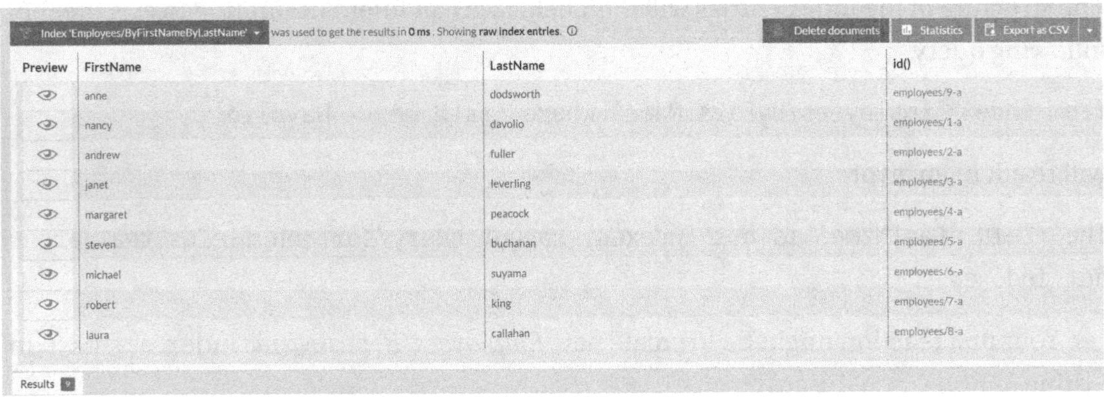

Preview	FirstName	LastName	id()
👁	anne	dodsworth	employees/9-a
👁	nancy	davolio	employees/1-a
👁	andrew	fuller	employees/2-a
👁	janet	leverling	employees/3-a
👁	margaret	peacock	employees/4-a
👁	steven	buchanan	employees/5-a
👁	michael	suyama	employees/6-a
👁	robert	king	employees/7-a
👁	laura	callahan	employees/8-a

Figure 5-4. *Raw Content of Index Employees/ByFirstNameByLastName*

You can query this new index both on the *FirstName* field

```
from index 'Employees/ByFirstNameByLastName' where FirstName = 'Nancy'
```

and on *LastName* field:

```
from index 'Employees/ByFirstNameByLastName' where LastName = 'Davolio'.
```

This way, you can use just one index to cover multiple fields of documents in one collection.

Indexing References

In the previous section, you saw how to create an index from the field that contained values – employees were indexed by their first name. Let's look at a slightly different scenario. If you open one of the orders, you will see they have references pointing to Company and Employee, as shown in Listing 5-6:

Listing 5-6. Order orders/830-A

```
{
    "Company": "companies/65-A",
    "Employee": "employees/1-A",
    "Freight": 8.53,
    "Lines": [
...
```

Following the same approach as we did for index *Employees/ByFirstName*, you can index *Orders* by the *Employee* field, presented in Listing 5-7:

Listing 5-7. Orders/ByEmployee index

```
map("Orders", order => {
    return {
        Employee: order.Employee
    }
})
```

Looking at indexing terms of this index, you can see identifiers of all employees extracted and indexed, as shown in Figure 5-5.

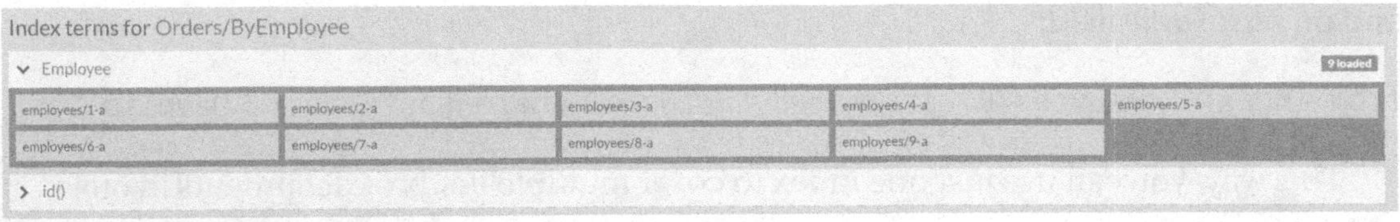

Figure 5-5. *Index Terms for Orders/ByEmployee Index*

Nancy Davolio's ID is *employees/1-A*, so you can query *Orders/ByEmployees* to get all of her orders:

```
from index 'Orders/ByEmployee' where Employee = 'employees/1-a'
```

However, it would be much more natural if you could query by Nancy Davolio's first name – that would not force you to check what her ID is. That would require an index to read an employee's id, load that document, and read FirstName property.

RavenDB provides function *load* that you can use to achieve that. Improved version of Oders/ByEmployee index is shown in Listing 5-8:

Listing 5-8. Orders/ByEmployeeName index

```
map("Orders", order => {
    var employee = load(order.Employee, 'Employees');
    return {
        EmployeeName: employee.FirstName
    }
})
```

You can now use this index to search orders by employee's first name:

```
from index 'Orders/ByEmployeeName' where EmployeeName = 'Nancy'
```

Inspecting Listing 5-8, you can see the usage of the *load* function:

```
load(order.Employee, 'Employees')
```

The first argument is the document's ID, and the second one is the document's collection.

This index will react to changes over Orders document collection and recalculate. Every time you call the load function in an index, RavenDB will note that your index depends not only on the collection it is indexing but also on the collection from which referenced documents are loaded. Since we are loading Employee documents, changes to that collection will also trigger updates to the index.

Stored Fields

In the previous chapter, we introduced different types of indexes: nonclustered (holding only references to documents), clustered (storing whole documents), and covering ones (including a selected collection of fields). Static indexes we developed so far in this chapter are nonclustered. You can easily inspect that by running the following query:

```
from index 'Employees/ByFirstNameByLastName'
```

After getting employee documents, click on *Settings* and select the option *Show stored index fields only*. You will get a result shown in Figure 5-6.

Figure 5-6. *No Stored Fields for Index Employees/ByFirstNameByLastName*

As you can see, an index does not contain any stored fields. So, when you run the query with a projection

```
from index 'Employees/ByFirstNameByLastName'
where FirstName = 'Nancy'
select FirstName, LastName
```

the database engine will first perform filtering based on an index, which will result in single ID *employees/1-A*. After that, the engine will make one more round trip to the storage to fetch this document and read its FirstName and LastName properties.

You can convert your nonclustered index into covering one by instructing RavenDB to store specific fields. Going back to the Index edit form and looking at the bottom of the screen, you can see the *Fields* tab in Figure 5-7.

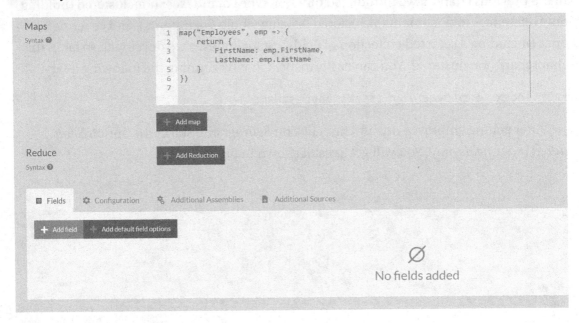

Figure 5-7. *Fields Tab on Edit Index Page*

This tab shows no fields added to the index. Add fields *FirstName* and *LastName* by clicking on Add field button, and populate both of their names, and select value Yes in the *Store* option, as shown in Figure 5-8.

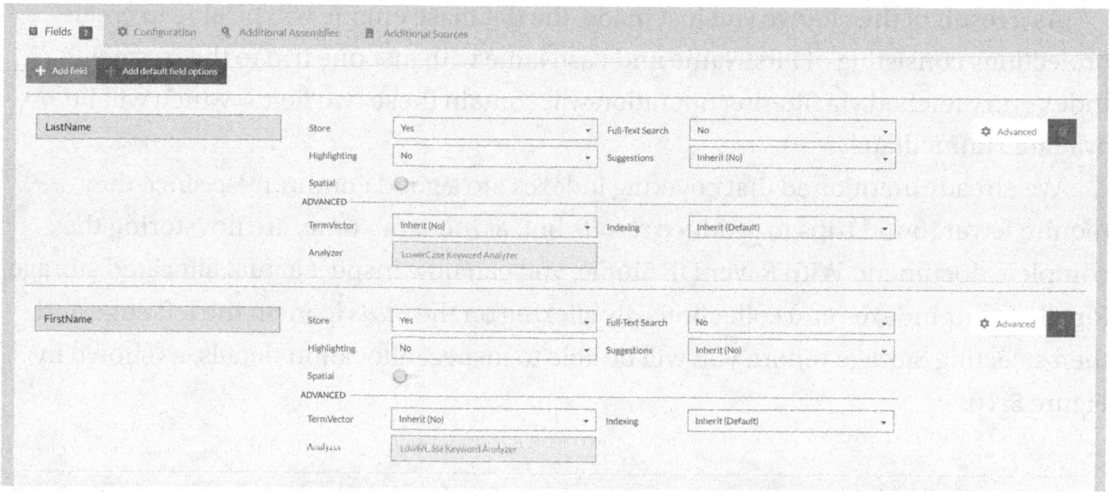

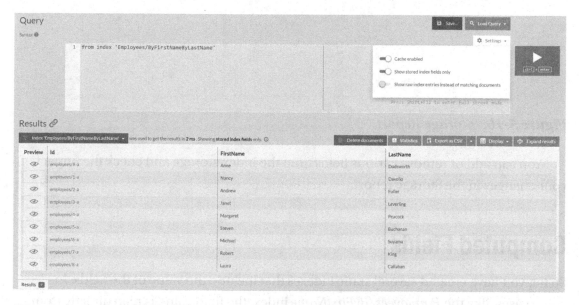

Figure 5-8. *Adding FirstName and LastName as Stored Fields in the Index*

After saving the changed index definition, repeating the query from Figure 5-6 will reveal stored fields of the *Employees/ByFirstNameByLastName* index, as presented in Figure 5-9.

Figure 5-9. *Stored Fields for Index Employees/ByFirstNameByLastName*

As a result of the change you just made, the database engine will be able to create projections consisting of FirstName and LastName with just one trip to the storage. Index entry fetched via filtering operation will contain these two fields, which will be available immediately.

We already mentioned that covering indexes are a good compromise since they require fewer round trips to produce results but, at the same time, are not storing the complete document. With RavenDB Studio, you can now inspect actual allocated storage for all of your indexes and collections. By clicking on the *Stats* icon on the left edge and then selecting Storage report, you will be able to inspect allocation details, as shown in Figure 5-10.

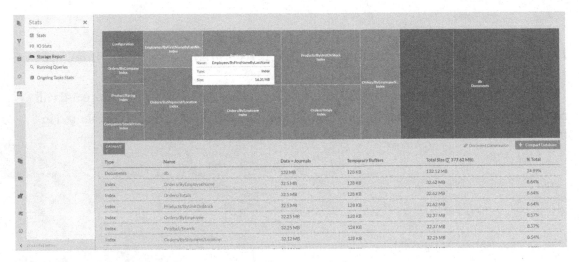

Figure 5-10. *Storage Report*

You can add or remove various fields from the index storage and check the impact of your changes in the Storage report.

Computed Fields

So far, you have created several static indexes that include the value of the fields. In some cases, like the *Employees/ByFirstName* index, the field value is read directly from processed documents. In others, like Orders/ByEmployeeName, a referenced document was loaded, and then the content of its field was indexed.

However, it is also possible to create index fields containing a value that does not exist in any documents. Such fields are called *computed fields*. We usually calculate their value based on one or more other fields.

Example of an index with computed field is shown in Listing 5-9.

Listing 5-9. Index Orders/ByEmployeeNameByTotal with Computed Field Total

```
map("Orders", order => {
    var employee = load(order.Employee, 'Employees');

    var total = 0;
    for (var i = 0; i < order.Lines.length; i++) {
        var line = order.Lines[i];
        total += line.Quantity * line.PricePerUnit * (1 - line.Discount);
    }

    return {
        EmployeeName: employee.FirstName,
        Total: total
    }
})
```

Index defined in Listing 5-9 is based on *Orders/ByEmployeeName* but expanded with field *Total*. Its value represents total monetary value of the order, and it is computed in the following way:

```
var total = 0;
for (var i = 0; i < order.Lines.length; i++) {
    var line = order.Lines[i];
    total += line.Quantity * line.PricePerUnit * (1 - line.Discount);
}
```

This is a relatively standard piece of imperative JS code. It iterates over *Order.Lines* array, and for every line, the total is `quantity * price * (1 - discount)`. Line totals are accumulated, and after lines are processed, variable *total* holds calculated total for Order.

You can use all features of JavaScript languages, like loops, functions, etc. You can even extract code into JS functions that will be called from the *map* function of an index, as shown in Listing 5-10.

Listing 5-10. Index Orders/ByEmployeeNameByTotal with functionality
extracted into JS function

```
function GetTotal(order) {
    var total = 0;

    for (var i = 0; i < order.Lines.length; i++) {
        var line = order.Lines[i];
        total += line.Quantity * line.PricePerUnit * (1 - line.Discount);
    }

    return total;
}

map("Orders", order => {
    var employee = load(order.Employee, 'Employees');

    return {
        EmployeeName: employee.FirstName,
        Total: GetTotal(order)
    }
})
```

It is also possible to use declarative style of JS, as shown in Listing 5-11.

Listing 5-11. Index Orders/ByEmployeeNameByTotal with declarative-style JS
function

```
function GetTotal(order) {
    return order.Lines.reduce((partial_sum, l) => partial_sum + (l.Quantity
    * l.PricePerUnit) * (1 - l.Discount), 0)
}

map("Orders", order => {
    var employee = load(order.Employee, 'Employees');

    return {
        EmployeeName: employee.FirstName,
        Total: GetTotal(order)
    }
})
```

It is also possible to embed business logic and business rules of your domain into index. Listing 5-12 gives one such example.

Listing 5-12. Index Orders/ByEmployeeNameByTotal expanded with business rules

```
function GetTotal(order) {
    var total = 0;

    for (var i = 0; i < order.Lines.length; i++) {
        var line = order.Lines[i];
        total += line.Quantity * line.PricePerUnit * (1 - line.Discount);
    }

    if (order.ShipTo.Country == "Poland") {
        total = 0.9 * total;
    }

    return total;
}

map("Orders", order => {
    var employee = load(order.Employee, 'Employees');

    return {
        EmployeeName: employee.FirstName,
        Total: GetTotal(order)
    }
})
```

We are giving a 10% discount to orders shipped to Poland, and that rule is embedded into the index as part of a computed field calculation.

Hence, now you can execute a query:

```
from index 'Orders/ByEmployeeNameByTotal'
where Total > 15000
```

to get all orders with a total monetary value of over 15,000.

So, with computed fields, you can create new properties calculated on existing properties with the application of possibly very complex logic. You can offload a significant portion of your business logic to a database if needed.

Dynamic Fields

As we mentioned earlier, RavenDB is a schemaless database. You do not have to define schema upfront, and you will be able to accept various semi-structured or even unstructured data. The moment you know least about your domain is the very moment when the project starts. The ability to postpone decisions about data structures you will use is a significant advantage. It will not just speed up development, but it will also provide much-needed flexibility as additional requirements arrive along the way of implementation and inevitably after you launch your product.

In other cases, you have very well-defined requirements, but the data you need to store inside a database is inherently heterogeneous. A typical situation is a need for globalization of your application. Expanding your business to a new part of the world often means learning about concepts you forgot to cover and modifying your application and database to take them into account.

Take the concept of an address as an example. Various countries around the world have different ways of addressing locations. It is enough to read multiple administrative division terms for countries worldwide – state, county, province, district, prefecture, emirate, canton, municipality, circuit, raion, oblast – to comprehend the full complexity of modeling such heterogeneous data.

Schemaless JSON as a data format for your documents in RavenDB will provide you with much-needed flexibility for expanding entities that you store. However, you need to propagate these changes to queries and the application itself. And, since queries are using indexes, you will also have to expand the RavenDB index definition. Once it's changed, this will trigger recomputation of the whole index, which can be both computation-heavy and time-consuming.

RavenDB provides a handy solution for situations like this one in the form of *dynamic fields*. Instead of explicitly stating field names and their values, you can programmatically define them. Such an index can accommodate different document structures. Also, dynamic fields will prevent complete recalculation of the index when a document with new fields arrives at the database. Listing 5-13 shows an index with dynamic fields generated for the employee's address.

Listing 5-13. Employees/DynamicFields index

```
function CreateDynamicFields(addr) {
    var ret = [];

    for (const property in addr) {
        ret.push(createField(property, addr[property], { indexing: 'Exact',
        storage: false, termVector: null }))
    }

    return ret;
}

map("Employees", emp => {
    return {
        _: CreateDynamicFields(emp.Address)
    }
})
```

As you can see from the *map* definition, this index is processing all employees and will create dynamic fields for their addresses. Listing 5-14 presents one sample address.

Listing 5-14. Address literal of employees/8-A

```
{
    "Line1": "4726 - 11th Ave. N.E.",
    "Line2": null,
    "City": "Seattle",
    "Region": "WA",
    "PostalCode": "98105",
    "Country": "USA",
    "Location": {
        "Latitude": 47.66416419999999,
        "Longitude": -122.3160148
    }
}
```

Figure 5-11 shows collections of index terms for addresses of this form.

Index terms for Employees/DynamicFields				
⌄ _				0 loaded
⌄ id()				9 loaded
employees/1-a	employees/2-a	employees/3-a	employees/4-a	employees/5-a
employees/6-a	employees/7-a	employees/8-a	employees/9-a	
› Line1 Dynamic field				
› Line2 Dynamic field				
⌄ City Dynamic field				5 loaded
kirkland	london	redmond	seattle	tacoma
› Region Dynamic field				
⌄ PostalCode Dynamic field				9 loaded
98033	98052	98105	98122	98401
ec2 7jr	rg1 9xp	sw1 8jr	wg2 7lt	
› Country Dynamic field				
› Location Dynamic field				

Figure 5-11. *Index Terms for Employees/DynamicFields Index*

Each property of the address (like Line1, Line2, City, etc.) is one collection of terms. Values of such group are extracted from all occurrences of that property on any of the employee documents.

Let's look at the definition of the index. You can see that definition of the dynamic field has a peculiar form:

```
_: CreateDynamicFields(emp.Address)
```

Underscore as an object literal name is just a convention. Figure 5-11 shows that a collection with the name _ will be created, but it does not have content.

Function that generates set of dynamic fields has the following definition:

```
function CreateDynamicFields(addr) {
    var ret = [];

    for (const property in addr) {
        ret.push(createField(property, addr[property], { indexing: 'Exact',
        storage: false, termVector: null }))
    }

    return ret;
}
```

An empty array is defined. The indexing engine will iterate over all address' properties and add a new dynamic field for every one of them.

RavenDB has built-in JS function:

```
createField(name, value, {options}).
```

You can use it to create a dynamic field `name:property`.

Note that the `CreateDynamicFields` function is entirely generic – no exact field names are stated. It can process any object literal passed to it, extract all property names and their values, and create dynamic fields for every property it finds.

Furthermore, modifying employee documents will trigger an index update, and a new field will be added to the indexing terms. As an exercise, open employee with id *employees/8-A* and expand its Address with the following property:

```
"Continent": "North America"
```

After saving changes, verify that a new index term collection with the name *Continent* has been created.

Overall, dynamic fields are a tool for creating flexible indexes which can process heterogeneous data and, at the same time, adapt to future changes your domain model might introduce.

Fanout Index

Indexes we created so far were processing documents and were creating one indexing entry per document. For example, index *Employees/ByFirstName* will take all nine employee documents, read their first name, and output one index entry per document. Figure 5-12 shows a summary for this index.

Figure 5-12. *Summary for Index Employees/ByFirstName*

Summary shows nine entries, one per document. The number of index entries equals number of documents in the collection.

It is possible to write an index which would output not one but multiple entries per processed documents. Such index is called *fanout index*. Listing 5-15 shows an example of such index.

Listing 5-15. Orders/ByProductName index

```
map('Orders', order => {
    var res = [];
    order.Lines.forEach(l => {
        res.push({
            ProductName: l.ProductName
        })
    });
    return res;
})
```

Fanout indexes can produce dozens, even hundreds, of entries per document. Index in Listing 5-15 iterates over all lines in every order and creates one indexing entry for each line. Every such entry contains a product name. Hence, for every order document, the index will create as many entries as there are order lines.

You are now able to find all orders containing the line with a specified product name:

```
from index 'Orders/ByProductName' where ProductName = 'chocolade'
```

Figure 5-13 shows that inspecting indexing entries for a specific order can reveal all of its entries and help you understand the fanout principle.

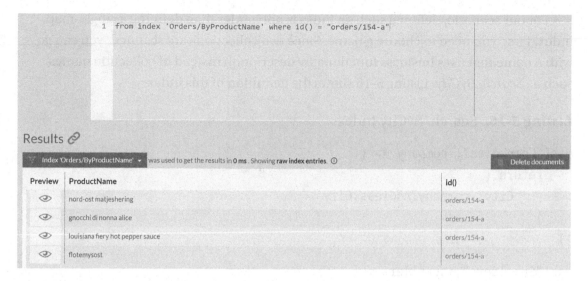

Figure 5-13. *Indexing Entries for Orders/154-a*

Going back to the index overview, you will see that this index contains 2,155 entries for 830 processed orders.

In the same manner, you can index all documents with embedded values.

Multi-Map Index

Up to this point, all indexes we defined were processing a single collection, loading properties of its documents, and extracting their values into indexing entries. However, it is not uncommon for documents in different collections to have the same properties. A typical example of this would be an address – in our sample dataset, Employees, Companies, and Suppliers all have this property.

Both Companies and Suppliers are legal entities, and it is not hard to imagine a business scenario where you would like to search both of them by city. One possible solution would be to create Companies/ByCity and Suppliers/ByCity indexes. However, you would have to perform two searches to get total results:

```
from index 'Companies/ByCity' where City = 'paris'
from index 'Suppliers/ByCity' where City = 'paris'
```

RavenDB provides a way to merge these two indexes into one. Such an index is called the *multi-map index*.

For our scenario, defining such an index is not harder than defining a single-map index. First, you need to choose a name. Since two collections are scanned, you can go with a name that uses business functionality description instead of collection names, such as *Search/ByCity*. Listing 5-16 shows the definition of this index.

Listing 5-16. Search/ByCity Index

```
map("Companies", company => {
    return {
        City: company.Address.City
    }
})

map("Suppliers", supplier => {
    return {
        City: supplier.Address.City
    }
})
```

You will add the first map as you usually do. Then, click on Add map button. One more text area will open so that you can add a second map definition. Your multi-map index is ready for querying, as shown in Figure 5-14.

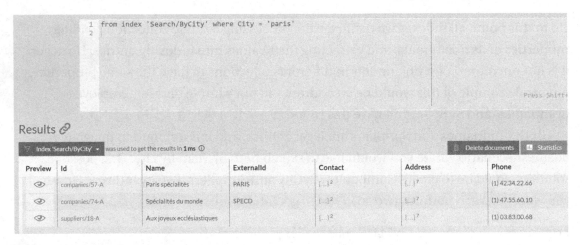

Figure 5-14. *Querying Multi-Map Search/ByCity Index*

The results you got are all companies and suppliers located in Paris.

You can expand this index with one more map that would process Employees. We will leave this as an exercise for you.

Indexing Hierarchical Data

Besides simple linear relations, your applications will inevitably need to represent and store more complex setups. One such structure is the hierarchy – chain of documents pointing to the next one sequentially. Typical representatives of hierarchical data are genealogical trees or threads of comments on a blog post.

Our sample database contains one example of hierarchical data, as shown in Listing 5-17.

Listing 5-17. ReportsTo property of employees/9-A document

```
{
    "LastName": "Dodsworth",
    "FirstName": "Anne",
    ...
    "ReportsTo": "employees/5-A",
    ...
```

Every employee has *ReportsTo* property that contains the identifier of another employee. In this chapter, you already saw examples of how to index related documents, so it is easy to come up with an index presented in Listing 5-18.

Listing 5-18. Employees/ByReportsToFirstName index

```
map("Employees", emp => {
    return {
        Manager : load(emp.ReportsTo, "Employees").FirstName
    }
})
```

Looking at index terms for this index, you can see it contains just two names: Andrew and Steven. Querying index for both of these names

```
from index 'Employees/ByReportsToFirstName' where Manager = 'Andrew'
from index 'Employees/ByReportsToFirstName' where Manager = 'Steven'
```

will reveal the structure of Northwind Traders company: Anne, Michael, and Robert report directly to Steven. Everyone else, including Steven, reports directly to Andrew. This hierarchy is also revealing itself in employee titles. Andrew is "Vice President, Sales" and Steven is "Sales Manager." All other employees bear "Sales Representative" and "Inside Sales Coordinator."

An important thing to notice here is Andrew's *ReportsTo* property:

```
"ReportsTo": null
```

This property is null, and *Employees/ByReportsToFirstName* will execute the following line:

```
load(null, "Employees").FirstName
```

However, unlike most programming languages, the null reference here will not create any problems. RavenDB will recognize an attempt to load a nonexisting document and handle that gracefully – it will not generate any indexing entries for Andrew. If you check the overview for this index, you will see that it has eight entries for nine processed employees.

The hierarchy we just computed is not a complete one – just direct superiors were fetched. After fetching a direct manager for every employee, we can continue climbing up the hierarchy tree until we reach the topmost manager in the hierarchy. Listing 5-19 defines an index that collects every employee's direct and indirect managers.

Listing 5-19. Employees/ByManagers index

```
map("Employees", empl => {
    if (empl.ReportsTo == null) return null;

    var managerNames = [];

    while (true) {
        empl = load(empl.ReportsTo, "Employees");
        if (empl == null)
            break;
```

```
        managerNames.push(empl.FirstName);
    }

    return {
        Manager: managerNames
    }
})
```

This index contains the same terms as a previous one (*Employees/ ByReportsToFirstName*), but indexing entries are different, as shown in Figure 5-15.

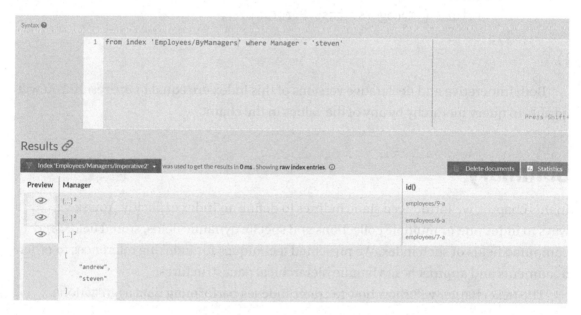

Figure 5-15. *Indexing Entries for Employees/ByManagers Index*

As you can see, we queried for all employees where a manager is Steven, and we got all three of them. However, index entries for these employees contain both Steven and Andrew – as we were looping up the hierarchy in Listing 5-19, Steven was added to an array, followed by Andrew, loaded as Steven's reporting officer.

Recursive nature of this index can be expressed in a declarative manner. RavenDB provides JS function recurse of the form

```
recurse(start_document, func(doc) -> doc)
```

which will start from a specified document and apply a `func` in a recursive way – returned document will be fed as an input to `func`. This chain of calls, defined in Listing 5-20, will continue up to the point when `func` returns null.

Listing 5-20. Recursive version of Employees/ByManagers index

```
map("Employees", empl => {
    var reportsTo = load(empl.ReportsTo, "Employees");
    return recurse(reportsTo, x => load(x.ReportsTo, "Employees"))
        .map(boss => {
            return { Managers: boss.FirstName };
        });
})
```

Both imperative and declarative versions of this index are equal in the result. You will be able to query hierarchy by any of the values in the chain.

Summary

In this chapter, we introduced static indexes to define an index explicitly. You saw ways to index one or multiple collections and specify dynamic fields, stored fields, and computed fields of such index. We presented techniques for indexing references to other documents and approaches to handle hierarchical data structures.

The next chapter will show how to create indexes performing data aggregations.

CHAPTER 6

MapReduce Indexes

The previous chapter demonstrated complete control over an index's definition and life cycle. Map and MultiMap indexes were introduced, along with various ways to compute fields that can be used to filter and sort documents. This chapter will show how to perform grouping and aggregation in RavenDB. Concepts of MapReduce and MultiMapReduce indexes will be introduced, along with a way to materialize the content of the index into a new collection.

Grouping

Queries executed in the previous chapter were about filtering. The filtering condition was defined, and the database returned all documents that matched it. Typical queries of this kind look like this:

```
from index 'Auto/Employees/ByFirstName'
where FirstName = 'Nancy'
```

or

```
from index 'Orders/ByEmployeeNameByTotal'
where Total > 15000
```

Besides filtering documents, RavenDB is also capable of grouping data. Let's say that we would like to analyze Orders by the shipping country. You can achieve that by running the query shown in Listing 6-1.

Listing 6-1. Grouping orders by the country of shipment

```
from Orders as o
group by o.ShipTo.Country
select o.ShipTo.Country
```

© Dejan Miličić 2022
D. Miličić, *Introducing RavenDB*, https://doi.org/10.1007/978-1-4842-8919-8_6

This query will result in a list of 21 different countries Northwind Traders sent orders to, as shown in Figure 6-1.

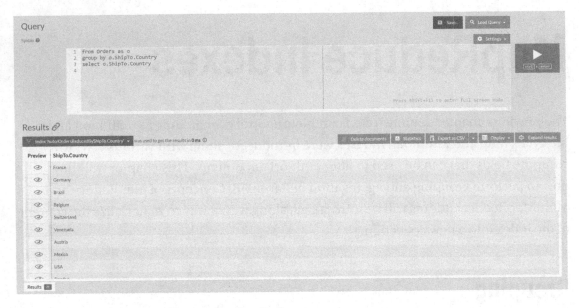

Figure 6-1. *Shipping Countries for Orders*

As with all previous queries you saw, this one also uses an index to return results. Since we did not define static one upfront, RavenDB created the automatic index *Auto/ OrdersReducedByShipTo.Country* which is visible in the listing of all indexes for your database. Clicking on it will reveal index details shown in Figure 6-2.

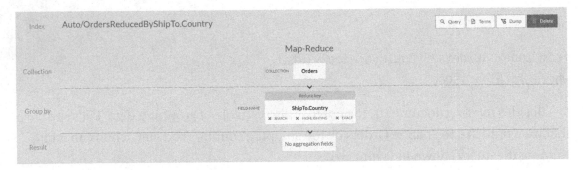

Figure 6-2. *Structure of Auto Index* Auto/OrdersReducedByShipTo.Country

Documents from Orders collection were processed, their *ShipTo.Country* values were extracted, and IDs of orders with the same values were stored in index entries. RavenDB uses a specific programming model we will examine in the next section for processing grouping tasks.

MapReduce

Figure 6-2 displays a visualization of the data grouping pipeline in an index. At the top of this diagram, you will see the *Map-Reduce* heading, denoting this index type. Alternatively spelled as *MapReduce*, this technique popularized by Google is used for the parallel processing of data across many machines. In a typical setup, data is first split into batches. Every batch is sent to a different device, which will use the *map* function to transform all entries in the received collection. Mapped entries are then combined via *reduce* function to produce the final result set.

The previous chapter saw examples of automatic and static indexes implementing map functions to transform documents into indexing entries. MapReduce index will take such mapped entries and apply reduce function to them, emitting grouped entries. RavenDB is using a variant of this programming model.

Unlike original MapReduce used at companies like Google, where data batches are distributed across hundreds and thousands of machines, RavenDB performs this process on a single machine. Multiple threads will receive packs, apply map function to emit projections first, and then apply reduce function to these projections.

RavenDB has a MapReduce visualizer that can help you examine MapReduce indexes. You can open it by clicking on the Indexes option in a sidebar, then the Map-Reduce Visualizer option, as shown in Figure 6-3. Understanding this process can be a bit tedious if this is the first time you are working with MapReduce or when you want to debug results over a large amount of data.

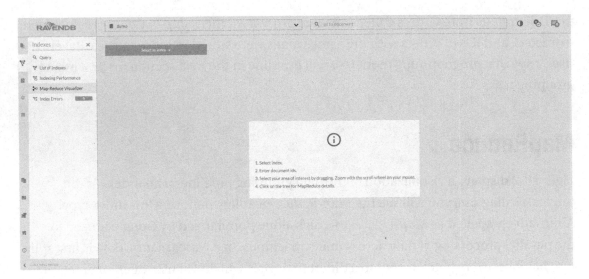

Figure 6-3. *Map-Reduce Visualizer Initial Screen*

On this screen, you can select the index your query created a moment ago, *Auto/OrdersReducedByShipTo.Country*, and select documents to present visualization for. Selecting orders/1-a and orders/103-a will generate representation as in Figure 6-4.

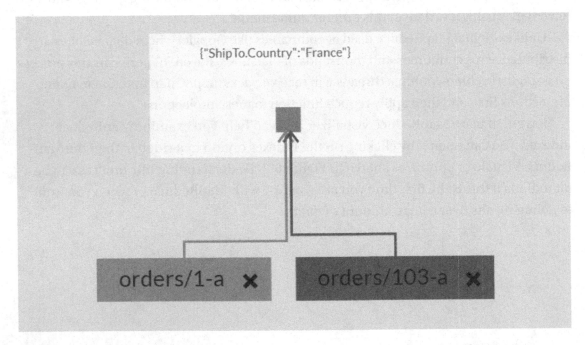

Figure 6-4. *Map-Reduce Visualization of Auto/OrdersReducedByShipTo.Country Index for orders/1-a and orders/103-a*

Map phase of the index extracted ShipTo.Country, while Reduce phase collected all orders with same shipping country. In Figure 6-4, you can see that the reduction phase gathered these two orders together since their shipping countries match. If you check the documents for these two orders, you will know that they went to France.

Clicking on the reduction box will expand the tree's root, as shown in Figure 6-5.

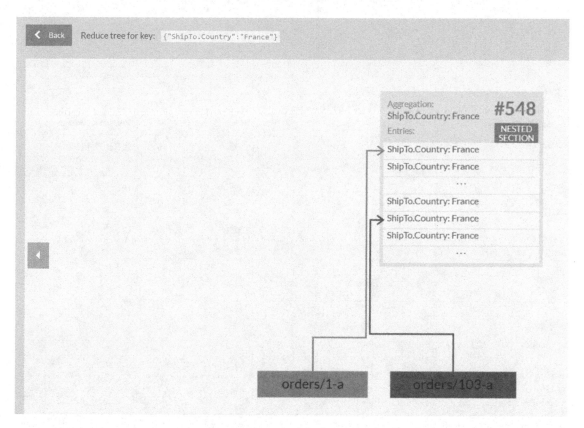

Figure 6-5. *Reduction Outcome Details*

You can see that the reduction phase grouped numerous orders shipped to France and that the two orders we selected are just two of many such orders. Clicking on the reduction box will show a scrollable listing of all these orders, as shown in Figure 6-6.

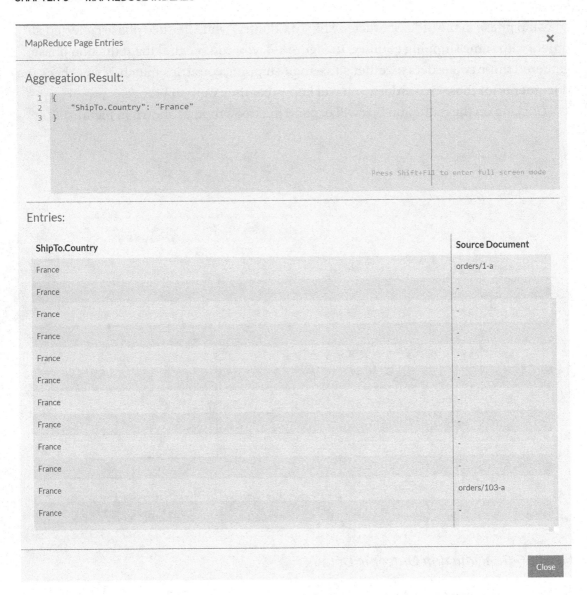

Figure 6-6. *Reducing Orders Shipped to France*

The ability for a database to perform groupings like this one is nice, but it is not too valuable. The full power of grouping comes with aggregation, which we will cover in the next section.

Aggregation

We started this chapter with a query shown in Listing 6-1. When executed, it will produce a list of shipping countries. However, we would like to see how many orders are shipped to these countries. Query returning that info is shown in Listing 6-2.

Listing 6-2. Grouping and counting orders by the country of shipment

```
from Orders as o
group by o.ShipTo.Country
select o.ShipTo.Country, count()
```

If you compare Listing 6-2 with the previous query in Listing 6-1, you can see that we expanded the select statement with *count()*. This query expansion will result in the addition of results, as shown in Figure 6-7.

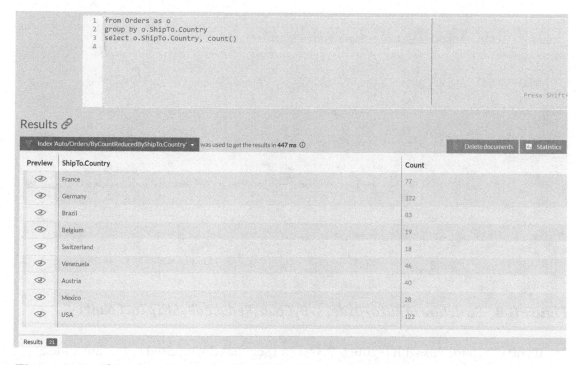

Figure 6-7. *Shipping Countries for Orders Expanded with Count*

Counts shown are calculated by applying the process of *aggregation* – calculating combined values for a group of results. In this case, RavenDB counted one for every order in a *country group* and came up with a total sum. Finally, we can execute this query:

```
from Orders as o
group by o.ShipTo.Country
order by count() as long desc
select o.ShipTo.Country, count()
```

and obtain a piece of useful information regarding the "Northwind Traders" business – most of their orders, 122, were delivered to customers in the United States and Germany.

As you can see, this query created the new automatic index `Auto/Orders/ByCountReducedByShipTo.Country`, and clicking on its name in the list of all indexes will reveal its internal structure, as shown in Figure 6-8.

Figure 6-8. *Structure of* `Auto/Orders/ByCountReducedByShipTo.Country`

If you compare this with Figure 6-2, you can see that the original automatic index was augmented with count operation in the aggregation phase.

Examining indexing terms for this index reveals fields with names `Count` and `ShipTo.Country`. These two aggregation categories provide us with a way to find out how many shipments went to Finland:

```
from index 'Auto/Orders/ByCountReducedByShipTo.Country'
where 'ShipTo.Country' = 'finland'
```

or to get a listing of all countries with more than 80 orders shipped to

```
from index 'Auto/Orders/ByCountReducedByShipTo.Country'
where 'Count' > 80
```

Static MapReduce Indexes

The previous chapter introduced the concept of static Map indexes. They are a natural extension of Map indexes, providing a way to map documents and then specify how to aggregate those maps. It is also possible to write static MapReduce indexes. This section will recreate a static version of automatic index `Auto/Orders/ByCountReducedByShipTo.Country`.

Start by creating map index, as shown in Listing 6-3:

Listing 6-3. `Orders/ByCountry` map index

```
map("Orders", order => {
    return {
        Country: order.ShipTo.Country
    }
})
```

This index is not much different from the `Employees/ByFirstName` index in the previous chapter – for every order document, RavenDB will create one indexing entry with Country value.

Final goal of this static index is to count totals, so let's expand mapping with numbers that you will aggregate later on, as in Listing 6-4:

Listing 6-4. Expanding `Orders/ByCountry` map index with count

```
map("Orders", order => {
    return {
        Country: order.ShipTo.Country,
        Count: 1
    }
})
```

Raw indexing entries for such expanded map index can be found in Figure 6-9.

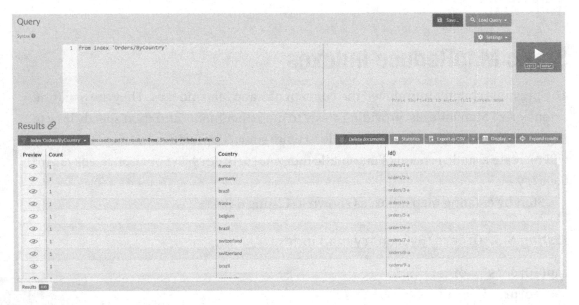

Figure 6-9. *Raw Indexing Entries for Expanded Map Index* `Orders/ByCountry`

This index is now performing the same task that you would do manually – going one by one order and writing down every occurrence of each country from ShipTo.Country field. After writing down marks of this kind for all orders, you would go back and sum it up. And that is precisely what the reduction phase of the MapReduce index does.

To add reduction script, open index for editing and click on Add Reduction button. New panel will open and you can add JS code for reducing all mappings that are emitted by map function. Code for this is visible in Listing 6-5:

Listing 6-5. Reduction code for index `Orders/ByCountry`

```
groupBy(map => map.Country)
    .aggregate(group => {
        var country = group.key;

        var count = 0;
        group.values.forEach(el => {
            count += el.Count;
        })

        return {
            Country: country,
            Count: count
        }
    })
```

Figure 6-10 shows the final form of the Orders/ByCountry MapReduce index.

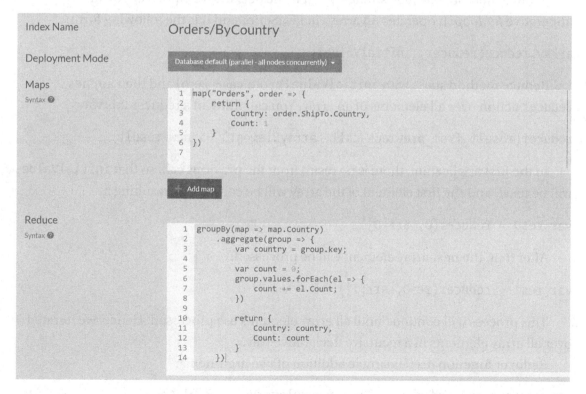

Figure 6-10. *MapReduce Index* `Orders/ByCountry`

Reduce script from Listing 6-5 can be refactored. Refactoring is the process of changing implementation without changing behavior. Let's reorganize the code to make it more concise.

First, you can replace imperative `forEach` loop defined in Listing 6-8 with functional equivalent based on *reduce* function:

```
groupBy(map => map.Country)
    .aggregate(group => {
        var country = group.key;
        var count = group.values.reduce((res, el) => res + el.Count, 0);

        return {
            Country: country,
            Count: count
        }
    })
```

Reduce method may look strange, but it is the declarative equivalent of an imperative *for loop*. It operates on arrays in JavaScript and has the following form:

```
array.reduce(reducer, initialValue);
```

Reduce method starts with `initialValue` (in our case, zero) and then applies reducer action over all elements of an array. You can think of a reducer this way:

```
reducer(result_from_previous_call, arrayElement) => new_result
```

In the first application, there is no result from the previous call, so that `initialValue` will be used, and the first element of the array will be consumed, resulting in

```
var res0 = reducer(0, arr[0])
```

After that, the next array element will be processed:

```
var res1 = reducer(res0, arr[1])
```

This process will continue until all array elements are processed. Hence, we iterated over all array elements in a recursive declarative way.

Reducer function itself is simple addition of two arguments:

```
reducer(accumulatedValue, el) = accumulatedValue + el.Count
```

As a second and final step in refactoring of reduction phase of our index, you can inline country and count variables:

```
groupBy(map => map.Country)
    .aggregate(group => {
        return {
            Country: group.key,
            Count: group.values.reduce((res, el) => res + el.Count, 0)
        }
    })
```

At this point, the automatic index `Auto/Orders/ByCountReducedByShipTo.Country` is replicated with static index `Orders/ByCountry`, so you can find out how many shipments went for Finland:

```
from index 'Orders/ByCountry'
where 'Country' = 'finland'
```

or to get a listing of all countries with more than 80 orders shipped to

```
from index 'Orders/ByCountry'
where 'Count' > 80
```

Static Versus Automatic Indexes

You just spent some effort implementing a static alternative to the index that was created automatically by RavenDB, and you may ask yourself, "why?" Indeed, if RavenDB can do the work on its own, what is the point?

There are several reasons why you would want to take control over index creation and its definition. Two of the most important reasons are discussed in the following sections.

Moment of Initial Indexing

Upon creating an index (both automatic and static), initial indexing will be performed. All documents will be fetched from the disk and processed by the index. If the indexed collection is empty, the newly created index will be ready immediately. However, if the collection is not empty, processing all documents will take a certain amount of time.

Executing query from Listing 6-1 will trigger the creation of an automatic index, and depending on the number of orders in the database, the initial indexing process may take a significant amount of time. While the indexing process is underway, the index will be *stale*. This means that the index contains many indexing entries, but this set is still incomplete. As a result, queries executed over the stale index may also return an incomplete result set. For example, following query

```
from index 'Auto/Orders/ByCountReducedByShipTo.Country'
where 'Count' > 80
```

might omit some countries because not all orders have been processed yet. In this situation, RavenDB may wait up to 15 seconds for the index to become nonstale. After 15 seconds, if the index is still stale, you will get partial results set, and indexing will continue in the background. The reasoning behind this decision is simple – instead of reporting an error, RavenDB will return a potentially incomplete result set with notification that some of the results might be missing.

In the production environment, you usually want to deploy or create indexes on live databases, wait for indexing processes to complete, and then deploy code using these new indexes.

With static indexes, you take more control over this process. Unlike automatic ones created on the first query, static indexes are explicitly defined. Hence, the indexing process will start after saving the static index definition. Overall, static indexes are more explicit and predictable, and you will create them intentionally before querying the database.

Aggregation Complexity

Query from Listing 6-2 that created automatic index `Auto/Orders/ByCountReducedByShipTo.Country` is doing aggregation by summing occurrences of orders with the same shipping country. Unfortunately, this simple aggregation is the limit of automatic MapReduce indexes. You will have to write a static MapReduce index for anything more advanced.

For example, we can follow up on the initial analysis of the count of orders by country and analyze the total value of the order by the country of shipment. However, by checking any of the orders in our sample database, you will see they are missing property with total monetary value. Instead of calculating this value and patching order documents, we can calculate it and store it as a part of an index, as shown in Listing 6-6:

Listing 6-6. Orders/ByCountryTotals index

```
map("Orders", order => {
    return {
        Country: order.ShipTo.Country,
        Total: order.Lines.reduce((total, line) => (line.Quantity * line.
        PricePerUnit) * (1 - line.Discount), 0)
    }
})

groupBy(map => map.Country)
    .aggregate(group => {
        return {
            Country: group.key,
            Total: group.values.reduce((res, el) => res + el.Total, 0)
        }
    })
```

The mapping phase of this index is processing order lines, taking into account line discount to compute the total value of each order. After that, these totals are summed up for a group of orders with the same shipping country.

You can now perform analysis like this one:

```
from index 'Orders/ByCountryTotals'
where Total > 50000
```

In this example, we applied complex aggregation and used its result as a part of our data model without altering documents in the database.

MultiMapReduce Indexes

Looking at companies we sell to and suppliers we buy from, you can perform the following two aggregations. In Listing 6-2, we analyzed orders by the country of shipping. Let's continue examining our dataset to explore the most active countries.

Countries where we sell

```
from "Companies" as c
group by c.Address.Country
select c.Address.Country, count()
```

Countries we buy from

```
from "Suppliers" as s
group by s.Address.Country
select s.Address.Country, count()
```

These two queries will return companies aggregated by countries and suppliers aggregated by countries. Additionally, these two queries will produce two automatic indexes. Manual aggregation of these two result sets will answer which countries Northwind Traders do the most business.

In the previous chapter, we covered the topic of MultiMap indexes, which are operating on more than one collection simultaneously. To write one static index that would replace two automatic ones, we can take MultiMap as a basis and then apply the reduction phase against generated projections. Such an index is called the *MultiMapReduce* index.

You start by defining two mapping phases of multi-map index Countries/Business as shown in Listing 6-7.

Listing 6-7. MultiMap index Countries/Business

```
map("Companies", company => {
    return {
        Country: company.Address.Country,
        Companies: 1,
        Suppliers: 0
    }
})
map("Suppliers", company => {
    return {
        Country: company.Address.Country,
```

```
        Companies: 0,
        Suppliers: 1
    }
})
```

If you compare this listing with Listing 6-4, you can see that we are counting again, but this time slightly modified. We need to count one for every company occurrence, but at the same time, we need to count events of suppliers as well.

RavenDB mandates all map functions you define within one index to have the same output. Hence, when counting companies, you also need to return suppliers and vice versa. To comply with this, you can use a simple approach – return data you are interested in, and for all other fields, return zero value. This will produce indexing entries, as shown in Figure 6-11.

Preview	Companies	Country	Suppliers	id()
👁	1	finland	0	companies/87-a
👁	1	brazil	0	companies/88-a
👁	1	usa	0	companies/89-a
👁	1	finland	0	companies/90-a
👁	1	poland	0	companies/91-a
👁	0	uk	1	suppliers/1-a
👁	0	usa	1	suppliers/2-a
👁	0	usa	1	suppliers/3-a
👁	0	japan	1	suppliers/4-a
👁	0	spain	1	suppliers/5-a

Figure 6-11. *Raw Indexing Entries of MultiMap Index* `Countries/Business`

As you can see, for every company and supplier document being processed, the index will extract its country, along with a count of one in an appropriate property.

All that is left to do now is to add aggregation. Hence, we expand the index with the reduction phase, which gives us the final form as shown in Listing 6-8.

Listing 6-8. MultiMapReduce index `Countries/Business`

```
map("Companies", company => {
    return {
        Country: company.Address.Country,
        Companies: 1,
```

```
        Suppliers: 0
    }
})

map("Suppliers", company => {
    return {
        Country: company.Address.Country,
        Companies: 0,
        Suppliers: 1
    }
})

groupBy(map => map.Country)
    .aggregate(group => {
        return {
            Country: group.key,
            Companies: group.values.reduce((res, el) => res +
            el.Companies, 0),
            Suppliers: group.values.reduce((res, el) => res +
            el.Suppliers, 0)
        }
    })
```

Finally, you can run the query:

```
from index 'Countries/Business'
```

to get a listing of countries with the number of companies and suppliers.

Artificial Documents

In addition to computing aggregations and storing them in an index, you can also materialize such indexing entries into documents called *artificial documents*. They will reside in a collection with an arbitrary name; every time the index is updated, this collection is also updated. This section will show scenarios when you want to create an artificial document, a walkthrough of their configuration, and to know how to perform indexing on them.

Querying index from Listing 6-8 will give raw indexing result as shown in Figure 6-12.

Country	Companies	Suppliers
Germany	11	3
Mexico	5	0
UK	7	2
Sweden	2	2
France	11	3
Spain	5	1
Canada	3	2
Argentina	3	0
Switzerland	2	0

Figure 6-12. *Raw Indexing Entries of Countries/Business Index*

You can now use these two fields of the index to order countries by the number of companies we do business with:

```
from index 'Countries/Business'
order by Companies as long desc
```

and by number of suppliers

```
from index 'Countries/Business'
order by Suppliers as long desc
```

However, what if we want to see totals? If you are making a business trip, which city would be your first choice? At which location would you have a chance to visit the most significant number of business entities your company is doing business with?

One way to solve this would be to expand index with additional field Total that would summarize Companies and Businesses, as shown in Listing 6-9.

Listing 6-9. Countries/Business Index Expanded with Total

```
map("Companies", company => {
    return {
        Country: company.Address.Country,
        Companies: 1,
```

```
            Suppliers: 0,
            Total: 1
        }
    })

map("Suppliers", company => {
    return {
        Country: company.Address.Country,
        Companies: 0,
        Suppliers: 1,
        Total: 1
    }
})

groupBy(map => map.Country)
    .aggregate(group => {
        return {
            Country: group.key,
            Companies: group.values.reduce((res, el) => res +
            el.Companies, 0),
            Suppliers: group.values.reduce((res, el) => res +
            el.Suppliers, 0),
            Total: group.values.reduce((res, el) => res + el.Total, 0)
        }
    })
```

With an expanded index, you can now query:

```
from index 'Countries/Business'
order by Total as long desc
```

to get desired information.

Instead of expanding the index, you might want to go with a query shown in Listing 6-10.

Listing 6-10. Querying index with a computed field

```
from index 'Countries/Business'
order by (Companies + Suppliers) as long desc
```

Executing this query will result in an error.

In Chapter 4, we talked about RavenDB's approach to indexing – all of your queries are always executed against indexes, and precomputed index entries are used to provide blazingly fast responses from the database. Under no circumstances can queries contain any computation. All such calculations must be done within the index itself, ahead of query time. Precisely for this reason, a query from Listing 6-10 will result in an error – we attempted to sum up `Companies` and `Suppliers` and then order countries based on that criterion. Revisiting the expanded index from Listing 6-9, you can see that we are performing totals summing in the indexing phase indeed.

Inspecting raw indexing entries of the index before expansion, shown in Figure 6-12, reveals a data structure that would be appropriate for writing a simple map index. Unfortunately, RavenDB indexes can operate only on documents, not on raw indexing entries within other indexes.

However, RavenDB provides a way to materialize raw indexing entries into actual documents, so you can query or even index them. In the next section, we will show how to achieve this.

Creating Artificial Documents

Start by returning index `Countries/Business` to the state from Listing 6-8 before expanding it with field `Total`. When you open the index for editing, right below *Reduce* script area, there is an *Output Reduce Results to Collection* option, as shown in Figure 6-13.

```
Reduce
Syntax ?
1  groupBy(map => map.Country)
2      .aggregate(group => {
3          return {
4              Country: group.key,
5              Companies: group.values.reduce((res, el) => res + el.Companies, 0),
6              Suppliers: group.values.reduce((res, el) => res + el.Suppliers, 0)
7          }
8      })
9
```

Output Reduce Results to Collection ①   CountriesBusiness

Create References to Results Collection ①

Figure 6-13. Outputting Index Reduce Results to CountriesBusiness Artificial Collection

As a result, raw index entries, the same one you can see in Figure 6-12, will be extracted and loaded into proper JSON documents. If you check the list of collections, you will notice a new one there – *CountriesBusiness* – as shown in Figure 6-14.

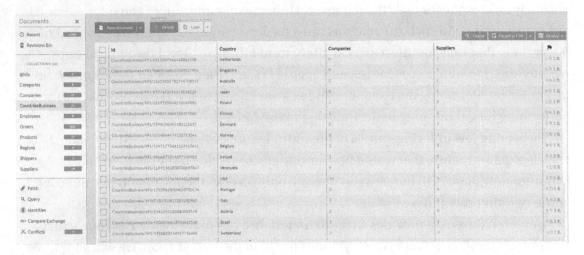

Figure 6-14. *Documents in the Artificial Collection CountriesBusiness*

This collection is called the *artificial collection*, and documents belonging to this collection are *artificial documents*. Opening one of these documents will reveal structure like one shown in Listing 6-11.

Listing 6-11. Structure of one artificial document

```
{
    "Country": "Finland",
    "Companies": 2,
    "Suppliers": 1,
    "@metadata": {
        "@collection": "CountriesBusiness",
        "@flags": "Artificial, FromIndex"
    }
}
```

Artificial documents can be created from MapReduce or MultiMapReduce indexes, containing indexing entries. If you compare raw indexing entries from Figure 6-12 with the content of the generated artificial collection, you will see that artificial collection represents a dump of an index. Artificial documents will contain all index fields as properties, and its metadata property will have a `flag` marking it as `Artificial, FromIndex`.

Every time a new order is created or an existing one is updated/deleted, all indexes indexing orders will be updated. The same thing will happen with the `Countries/Business` index, and its aggregated entries will be incrementally updated to take into account the latest changes. Additionally, since `Countries/Business` has output collection defined, this artificial collection will be updated.

Besides being automatically created by RavenDB, artificial documents are completely normal documents. Hence, you can run queries like

```
from 'CountriesBusiness'
where Country = 'UK'
```

to get number of companies and suppliers from the United Kingdom and

```
from 'CountriesBusiness'
where Companies > 1 and Suppliers > 1
select Country
```

to get a list of countries with at least one Company and Supplier.

Indexing Artificial Documents

After executing two queries from the previous section, you will discover that RavenDB created automatic index `Auto/CountriesBusiness/ByCompaniesAndCountryAndSuppliers`, which is expected behavior from your database.

Artificial documents are completely regular documents, so it is also possible to write Map or even MapReduce indexes which would process and aggregate them if needed. Hence to answer our original quest of finding countries with most suppliers and companies, we can first start by defining Map index `CountriesBusiness/Totals`, as shown in Listing 6-12.

Listing 6-12. CountriesBusiness/Totals index

```
map("CountriesBusiness", entry => {
    return {
        Country: entry.Country,
        Total: entry.Companies + entry.Suppliers
    }
})
```

You can now finally execute a query that will produce a list of countries, ordered by business activities in descending order:

```
from index 'CountriesBusiness/Totals'
order by Total as long desc
select Country
```

It is easy to see that your next business trip should be to the United States, Germany, and France.

Summary

This chapter introduced MapReduce and MultiMapReduce indexes to group and aggregate data. We introduced techniques for writing static versions of these indexes, along with a way to materialize their content into artificial documents. The next chapter will show how you can use RavenDB for full-text searching of your data.

CHAPTER 7

Full-Text Search

We already mentioned the full-text search capabilities of RavenDB in Chapter 3, and this chapter will expand on the concepts introduced there. We will show basic search capabilities, including operators, wildcards, and ranking. You will learn what lies under the hood and how RavenDB indexes process text internally to provide all these capabilities. Finally, we will demonstrate how you can take more control over the indexing process and apply advanced techniques with static indexes.

Basics of Full-Text Search

Looking at standard features in modern applications, you will quickly realize that ability to perform a full-text search is high on this list. Almost every application needs it. With a large amount of data, the ability to search becomes crucial; information that is not readily retrievable is essentially unusable.

In previous chapters, we saw how to perform filtering based on the exact match – you would specify the property name and value, and the database would return one or more documents where a property has that value.

The beauty of full-text search is partial matching – you can search for a particular term that is part of a text. For example, you can locate all books with a title containing "London" or all products with "chocolate" in the name. You can also specify prefixes or suffixes and get all matching documents. It is possible to pass multiple terms, and the database will return a union of documents containing any of those terms.

Let's look at various ways you can search text with RavenDB.

© Dejan Miličić 2022
D. Miličić, *Introducing RavenDB*, https://doi.org/10.1007/978-1-4842-8919-8_7

Single Term

As you can see in Figure 7-1, sample database products' names consist of one or more words.

Id	Name
products/77-A	Original Frankfurter grüne Soße
products/76-A	Lakkalikööri
products/75-A	Rhönbräu Klosterbier
products/74-A	Longlife Tofu
products/73-A	Röd Kaviar
products/72-A	Mozzarella di Giovanni
products/71-A	Flotemysost
products/70-A	Outback Lager
products/69-A	Gudbrandsdalsost
products/68-A	Scottish Longbreads
products/67-A	Laughing Lumberjack Lager

Figure 7-1. *Names of Products*

You can search for tofu products:

```
from "Products"
where search(Name, 'Tofu')
```

This query will return products with the names *Tofu* and *Longlife Tofu*. A term you search for can be at the beginning, the end, or anywhere inside the product name; RavenDB will easily match any position.

Note that the following query will produce identical results.

```
from "Products"
where search(Name, 'tofu')
```

With default settings, the full-text search feature in RavenDB is case insensitive.

Before performing a search, RavenDB will normalize the term by removing special and interpunction characters. As a result, all of these terms will produce identical results:

- "tofu"

- " tofu "

- "-tofu,"

Multiple Terms

You can search for multiple terms:

```
from "Products"
where search(Name, 'tofu vegie')
```

This query will produce results you can see in Figure 7-2.

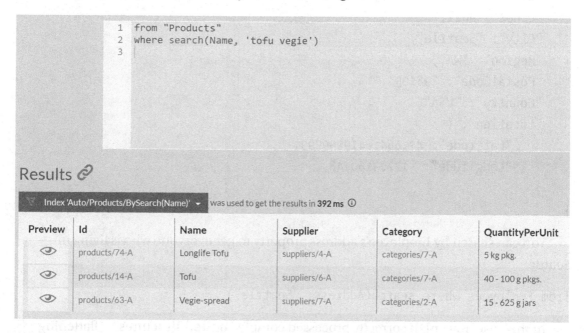

```
1  from "Products"
2  where search(Name, 'tofu vegie')
3
```

Results 🔗

Index 'Auto/Products/BySearch(Name)' ▾   was used to get the results in **392 ms** ⓘ

Preview	Id	Name	Supplier	Category	QuantityPerUnit
👁	products/74-A	Longlife Tofu	suppliers/4-A	categories/7-A	5 kg pkg.
👁	products/14-A	Tofu	suppliers/6-A	categories/7-A	40 - 100 g pkgs.
👁	products/63-A	Vegie-spread	suppliers/7-A	categories/2-A	15 - 625 g jars

Figure 7-2. *Search Results for the Terms "tofu vegie"*

This query will return all products with "tofu" or "vegie" in the name. You can expand this further, adding additional terms:

```
from "Products"
where search(Name, 'tofu vegie chocolade')
```

thus, including products containing any of these terms in the Name property.

Searching over Complex Objects

RavenDB can search not just over simple text fields but also over compound ones. The structure of an employee address is JSON, like the one in Listing 7-1.

Listing 7-1. A nested structure of Address property of Employee document

```
"Address": {
    "Line1": "4726 - 11th Ave. N.E.",
    "Line2": null,
    "City": "Seattle",
    "Region": "WA",
    "PostalCode": "98105",
    "Country": "USA",
    "Location": {
        "Latitude": 47.66416419999999,
        "Longitude": -122.3160148
    }
}
```

You can search by Employee's address property to get everyone who is living in Seattle:

```
from Employees where search(Address, "Seattle")
```

In this case, RavenDB correctly processed complex nested structures by flattening them and indexing all properties from various levels.

Searching over collections is supported as well. Orders in our sample database contain a collection of order lines. You can search for all orders containing fried products with the following query:

```
from Orders
where search(Lines.ProductName, "Fried")
```

Wildcards

Partial matching of full-text search provides a way to specify a word for searching within the text. Wildcards can increase the power of partial searching – you can replace one or more letters in situations where the beginning or end of a search term is unknown.

Hence, instead of searching for all employees named *Anne*

```
from "Employees"
where search(FirstName, 'Anne')
```

you can use a wildcard to specify just a portion of the search term. The following query will search for any first names with *An* prefix.

```
from "Employees"
where search(FirstName, 'An*')
```

Executing this query will return *Andrew* and *Anne*.

Accordingly, you can perform a suffix search:

```
from "Employees"
where search(LastName, '*an')
```

This query will return Steven Buchanan and Laura Callahan from our sample dataset.

Finally, combining the previous two approaches, we can execute an infix search:

```
from "Employees"
where search(FirstName, '*an*')
```

This infix full-text search will return *Anne*, *Nancy*, *Andrew*, and *Janet*.

When using wildcards, one more critical factor to consider is performance. Using a leading wildcard drastically slows down searching. Of course, this slowdown will not be significant on small datasets (like the current sample dataset we are using). Still, it may become a factor as the number of documents in your database increases. Hence, you should bear that in mind and evaluate every suffix full-text search scenario, both for justification and for potential negative impact.

If you nevertheless determine that your application needs this type of searching, there are a couple of alternatives:

- Create a static index where you would index reversed text, thus transforming leading wildcard searches (search by suffix) into trailing wildcard searches (search by prefix).

- Create a static index with a non-default analyzer.

Later in this chapter, we will cover the second technique.

Suggestions

Sometimes, the search will return no results. For example, none of the products contain the word "chaig" in the name, which can be verified by executing the following query:

```
from Products
where search('Name', 'chaig')
```

In such situations, RavenDB offers *suggest* feature. You can use it by calling suggest() function, like in Listing 7-2.

Listing 7-2. Selecting suggestions

```
from Products
select suggest('Name', 'chaig')
```

Executing this query will return suggestions shown in Figure 7-3.

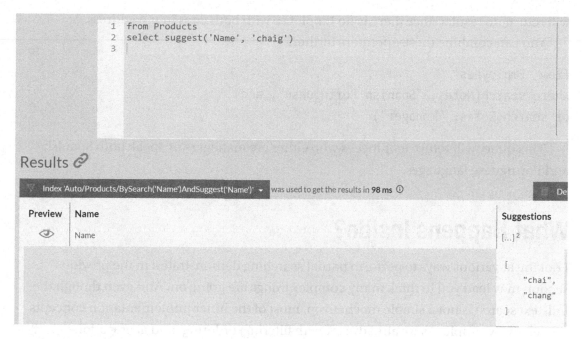

Figure 7-3. Suggestions for the Word "chaig"

Suggest function will find words similar to the term passed, based on the calculated distance algorithm value. This is handy if you want to implement Google-style "Did you mean?" suggestions.

Operators

We already showed that you could use more than one term for a full-text search, and you will get all documents satisfying one or the other. Essentially, RavenDB will implicitly apply the *or* logical operator. This means that query

```
from Employees where search(Address, "Seattle London")
```

is equivalent to

```
from Employees where search(Address, "Seattle London", or)
```

and will return all employees living either in Seattle or London.

Applying *and* operator

```
from Employees where search(Address, "Seattle London", and)
```

will return no results since there is no Employee with both cites in the address.

You can combine these operators further:

```
from 'Employees'
where search(Notes, "Spanish Portuguese", and)
or search(Notes, "Manager")
```

This query will return employees who either are managers or speak both Spanish and Portuguese languages.

What Happens Inside?

Looking at various ways to perform partial searching demonstrated in the previous section may lead you to think many complex things are going on. And even though the full-text search is not a simple mechanism, most of the inner implementation concepts are relatively simple. As we already saw with filtering, ordering, and aggregations - it all comes down to using appropriate data structures. Next, to avoid computation during query time, which is always dangerous since the query's execution time depends on the dataset's size, RavenDb will prepare index entries upfront. As a result, full-text search is efficient and fast. A certain amount of work is imminent, but doing it at most once, ahead of time, and storing the outcome for reuse is the key to performant queries.

Text Analysis

During indexing, RavenDB will use an analyzer to separate text into segments. These segments are called *tokens*, and they will form index terms. Later, when you perform a full-text search, your search term is matched against tokens contained in an index. Hence, this approach will transform a partial match of a search term against text into an exact match against the collection of tokens produced during the analysis of the text. Of course, this statement simplifies the whole process but conceptually describes the matching mechanism well.

Primarily, the analyzer performs *tokenization* of the text. Tokenization breaks text into lexical units, also called tokens. Tokens are the shortest searchable units, and the tokenization process converts input text into a token stream.

Additionally, tokens produced by a tokenizer are passed through one or more *filters*. Filters will examine the token stream and may leave tokens intact, modify them, discard them, or even create new ones. Alterations may include normalizing characters to all lower case or a version without diacritics. Punctuation and stop words like *the* and *is* are often removed, as are other unhelpful tokens that might impact the search quality.

Tokenizers and filters are usually combined into a pipeline (also called chain sometimes) where the output of one is input for another. The analyzer is simply a term for a sequence of tokenizers and filters that take text as input and produce a set of tokens.

Standard Analyzer

RavenDB comes with several analyzers, with *Standard Analyzer* as a default one. Standard Analyzer consists of *Standard Tokenizer* and two filters – *LowercaseToken Filter* and *StopToken Filter*.

Standard Tokenizer will perform segmentation of text by treating whitespaces, newlines, interpunction, and other special characters as token boundaries. Such generated stream of tokens is passed through LowercaseToken Filter, which will normalize them to all small letters. Finally, StopToken Filter will remove English *stop words* from the token stream. Examples are *a*, *the*, and *is* – these are so-called *function words*, which are ambiguous or have little lexical meaning in the context of full-text search.

As an example, the following sentence

```
A quick Fox jumps over the lazy Dog!
```

passed through Standard Analyzer will be transformed into a stream of tokens:

```
[quick], [fox], [jumps], [over], [lazy], [dog]
```

This process will remove exclamation marks and common words like *a* and *the*. Additionally, all tokens are lowercased.

As we have seen in previous chapters, running various queries will trigger RavenDB to create appropriate indexes to serve those queries efficiently. Likewise, RavenDB will create an automatic full-text search index when you run a full-text search query. Standard Analyzer will be applied to one or more searched fields. Their content will be tokenized, and a set of index entries will be generated.

An interesting fact is that Analyzer will not only be applied to input text during indexing but also to search terms. So, when executing a query

```
from "Employees"
where search(FirstName, 'Andrew Anne')
```

RavenDB will apply Standard Analyzer to string "Andrew Anne" transforming it into a token stream [andrew], [anne] and only then perform actual matching of these tokens to indexing terms. This rule has one exception – if a search term contains a wildcard, it will remain. An analyzer is not applied to search terms containing wildcards.

Besides Standard, RavenDB comes with additional analyzers:

- Keyword Analyzer

- LowerCase Whitespace Analyzer

- NGram Analyzer

- Simple Analyzer

- Stop Analyzer

- Whitespace Analyzer

You can use some of these to populate your full-text search index with differently shaped tokens. We will cover one such case later in this chapter.

Finally, RavenDB supports custom analyzers. Depending on the circumstances, you may have specific needs for tokenization and filtering. In such situations, you can write your custom analyzer and supply it to RavenDB. A typical example is the analysis of content in different languages. You can already guess that set of stop words is language-dependent. For example, the English word *car* is among the stop words in the French language. Custom analyzers are out of the scope of this book, but it is good to be aware of the highly customizable nature of RavenDB.

Ranking

For full-text search results to be helpful and for users of your application to be satisfied, most relevant results should be ranked at the top, followed by less relevant results. How does RavenDB determine relevancy?

Let's look at some examples.

Running query

```
from Employees where search(Address, "Seattle Redmond")
select Address.City
```

you will see that two employees from Seattle are positioned first, followed by a single one from Redmond. If we change the order of cities to

```
from Employees where search(Address, "Redmond Seattle")
select Address.City
```

you will notice results are sorted in reverse order compared to the previous query, following the order of search terms – first employee from Redmond and then two from Seattle.

As you can observe, this ordering is not a random one. RavenDB orders search results based on relevancy, so users are more likely to see more relevant results at the top of the list. When searching for "Redmond Seattle," RavenDB will consider the first search term more important than the second one, so employees from Redmond will be ranked before employees from Seattle. You can introduce additional search terms as we did in Listing 7-3.

Listing 7-3. Searching for multiple terms

```
from Employees where search(Address, "London Seattle Redmond")
select Address.City
```

This query will rank London employees first and then Seattle employees, and finally, any Redmond employees will be at the bottom of the list.

For every full-text search match, RavenDB computes the indexing score and uses it to determine the ranking of the results. This score is contained in the @index-score property within the @metadata of every search result. You can inspect it by previewing any results from a query from Listing 7-3, as shown in Figure 7-4. @index-score is the last property of @metadata.

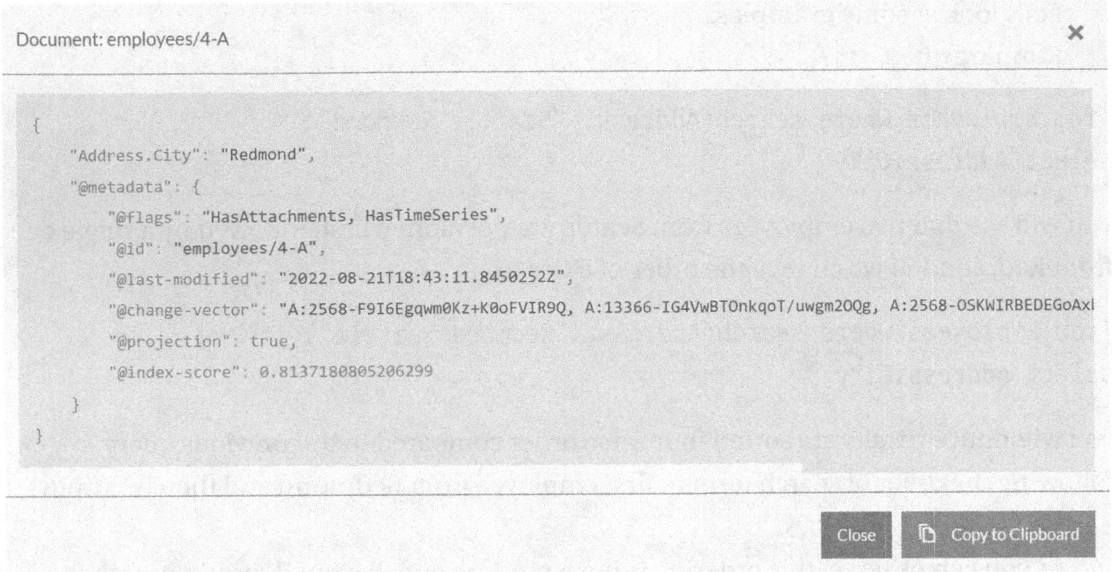

Figure 7-4. *The Indexing Score Located Within the Metadata*

The larger the @index-score is, the more relevant result will be. Indexing score is exposed via `score()` function. Hence, a query from Listing 7-3 is functionally equivalent to the following query:

```
from Employees where search(Address, "London Seattle Redmond")
order by score() desc
select Address.City
```

You can use the `score()` function to reverse ranking and show the least relevant results first if you need:

```
from Employees where search(Address, "London Seattle Redmond")
order by score() asc
select Address.City
```

RavenDB can also give you a detailed explanation of how it calculates the score. Along with the query, include the `explanations()` function, like in the following query:

```
from Employees where search(Address, "Redmond Seattle")
select Address.City
include explanations()
```

This time, query results are accompanied by ranking scores in an additional tab, as shown in Figure 7-5.

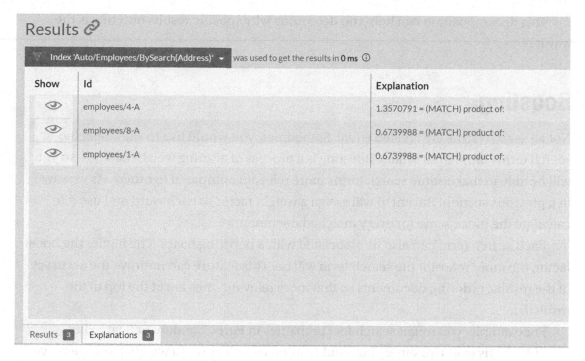

Figure 7-5. *Explanation Column with Ranking Scores*

Clicking on the *Show* icon will give you a detailed explanation of how the indexing score was computed, as shown in Figure 7-6.

Figure 7-6. *A Detailed Explanation of the Indexing Score*

This decomposition can help you determine why specific results ordering is the way it is.

Boosting

Not all search terms are created equal. Sometimes, you would like to value specific search terms more than others. Boosting is a process of altering weight factors – so you will be able to make some search terms more relevant compared to others. As we saw in a previous section, RavenDB will assign a weight factor to each word and use it to calculate the index score for every matched document.

Each search term can also be associated with a boosting factor. The higher the boost factor, the more relevant the search term will be. This feature can improve the accuracy of the results, ordering documents so that more relevant ones are at the top of the result list.

For example, you might search for companies in Paris, London, or Seattle but prioritize Paris over two other cities and London over Seattle. To write such a query, you can leverage the boost() function, which accepts boosting factor as a second argument, as shown in Listing 7-4.

Listing 7-4. Full-text search query with boost() function applied

```
from Companies
where
    boost(search(Address.City, 'paris'), 15) or
    boost(search(Address.City, 'london'), 10) or
    boost(search(Address.City, 'seattle'), 5)
select Address.City
```

After executing the query from Listing 7-4, RavenDB will return companies from these three cities, ranking as in Figure 7-7.

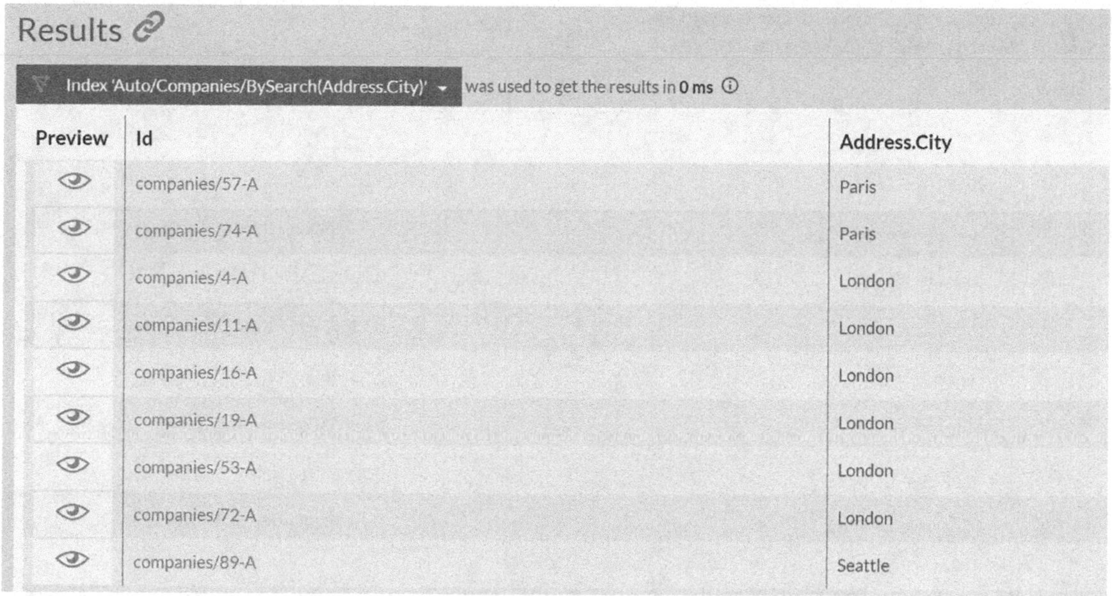

Results 🔗

Index 'Auto/Companies/BySearch(Address.City)' ▾   was used to get the results in **0 ms** ⓘ

Preview	Id	Address.City
👁	companies/57-A	Paris
👁	companies/74-A	Paris
👁	companies/4-A	London
👁	companies/11-A	London
👁	companies/16-A	London
👁	companies/19-A	London
👁	companies/53-A	London
👁	companies/72-A	London
👁	companies/89-A	Seattle

Figure 7-7. *Result Ordering Modified with boost() Function*

You can expand the query from Listing 7-4 with explanations, as shown in Listing 7-5.

Listing 7-5. Boosting query with included explanations

```
from Companies
where
    boost(search(Address.City, 'paris'), 15) or
    boost(search(Address.City, 'london'), 10) or
    boost(search(Address.City, 'seattle'), 5)
select Address.City
include explanations()
```

With such an expanded query, you will have an overview of scores visible in Figure 7-8.

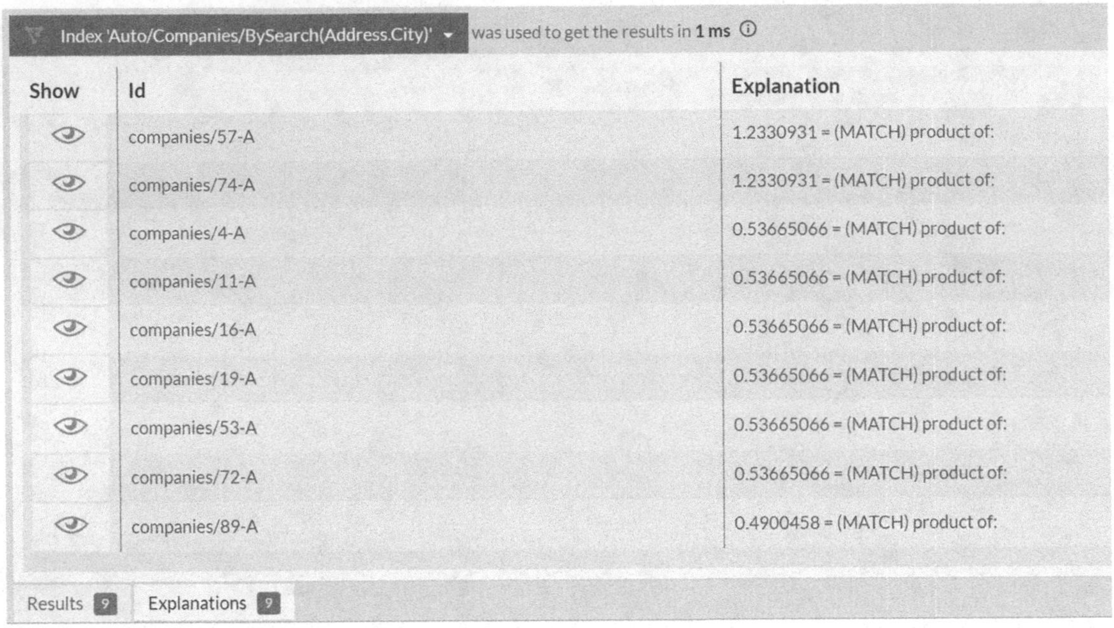

Show	Id	Explanation
👁	companies/57-A	1.2330931 = (MATCH) product of:
👁	companies/74-A	1.2330931 = (MATCH) product of:
👁	companies/4-A	0.53665066 = (MATCH) product of:
👁	companies/11-A	0.53665066 = (MATCH) product of:
👁	companies/16-A	0.53665066 = (MATCH) product of:
👁	companies/19-A	0.53665066 = (MATCH) product of:
👁	companies/53-A	0.53665066 = (MATCH) product of:
👁	companies/72-A	0.53665066 = (MATCH) product of:
👁	companies/89-A	0.4900458 = (MATCH) product of:

Index 'Auto/Companies/BySearch(Address.City)' ▾ was used to get the results in **1 ms** ⓘ

Results 9   Explanations 9

Figure 7-8. Explanation Tab with Computed Scores

You can click on the Show icon for a further breakdown of how these scores were calculated.

One more possibility to leverage boosting is to make specific fields more relevant. For example, we might need to locate all employees with managerial capabilities. A good candidate for searching is *Title* and *Notes* field. However, these two fields are substantially different – while Title contains a current position with the company, Notes contains an employee's description that may mention various skills and previous jobs. Employees in current managerial positions are more relevant than those with administrative functions in the past.

Hence, we can express that in a query from Listing 7-6.

Listing 7-6. Boosting of Title over Notes

```
from "Employees"
where boost(search(Title, 'manager'), 2)
or search(Notes, 'manager')
```

Results of execution are visible in Figure 7-9.

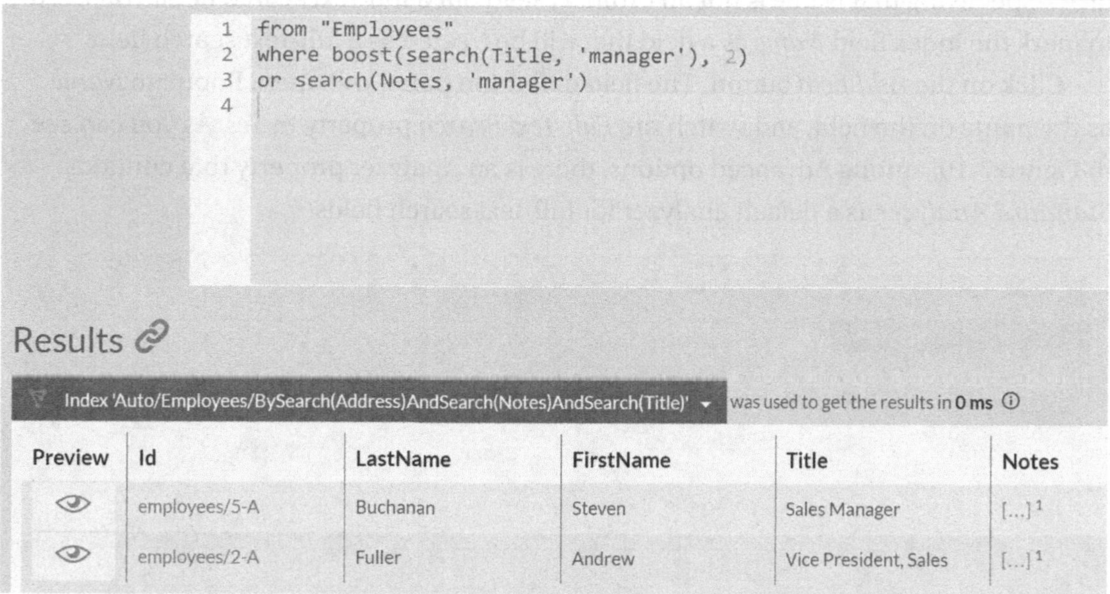

```
1  from "Employees"
2  where boost(search(Title, 'manager'), 2)
3  or search(Notes, 'manager')
4
```

Results &

Index 'Auto/Employees/BySearch(Address)AndSearch(Notes)AndSearch(Title)' ▾   was used to get the results in **0 ms** ⓘ

Preview	Id	LastName	FirstName	Title	Notes
👁	employees/5-A	Buchanan	Steven	Sales Manager	[...] [1]
👁	employees/2-A	Fuller	Andrew	Vice President, Sales	[...] [1]

Figure 7-9. *Results of Boosting Title over Notes*

As you can see, Steven is ranked higher than Andrew since he has the word Manager in the Title field. Using this approach, you can fine-tune ranking and provide better accuracy.

Static Index: One Field

We can take more control over the indexing process by switching from automatic indexes to static ones. You already learned how to create static indexes in Chapters 5 and 6. Listing 7-7 shows a simple index for searching over product names.

Listing 7-7. Products/ByName index

```
map("Products", function(product) {
    return {
        Name: product.Name
    }
})
```

Before saving the definition of this new index, there is one more step you need to take – specifying that Name is not an ordinary field but a full-text search field. You need to mark the index field *Name* as a field that will be treated as a full-text search field.

Click on the *Add field* button. The field definition panel will open. Populate *Name* as the name on the field, and switch the *Full-Text Search* property to *Yes*. As you can see in Figure 7-10, among Advanced options, there is an Analyzer property that contains *Standard Analyzer* as a default analyzer for full-text search fields.

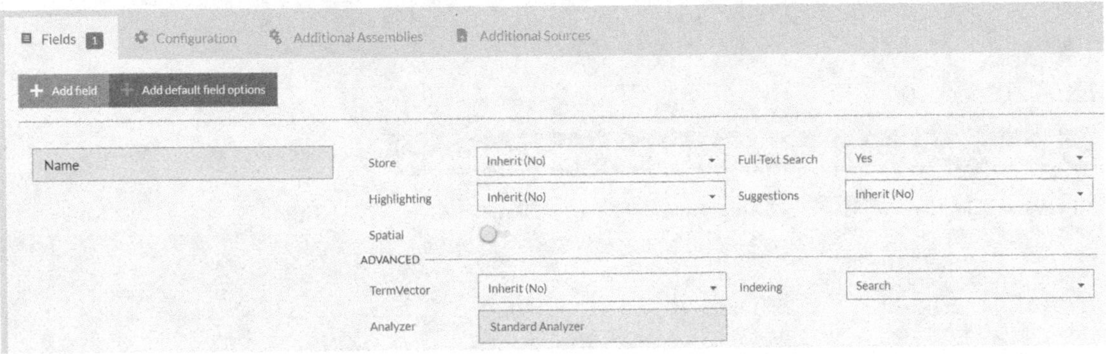

Figure 7-10. *Field Options*

After saving the definition of this new index, RavenDB will process all documents from the Products collection, extract the value of their Name property, and apply Standard Analyzer to tokenize product names. You can see index terms in Figure 7-11.

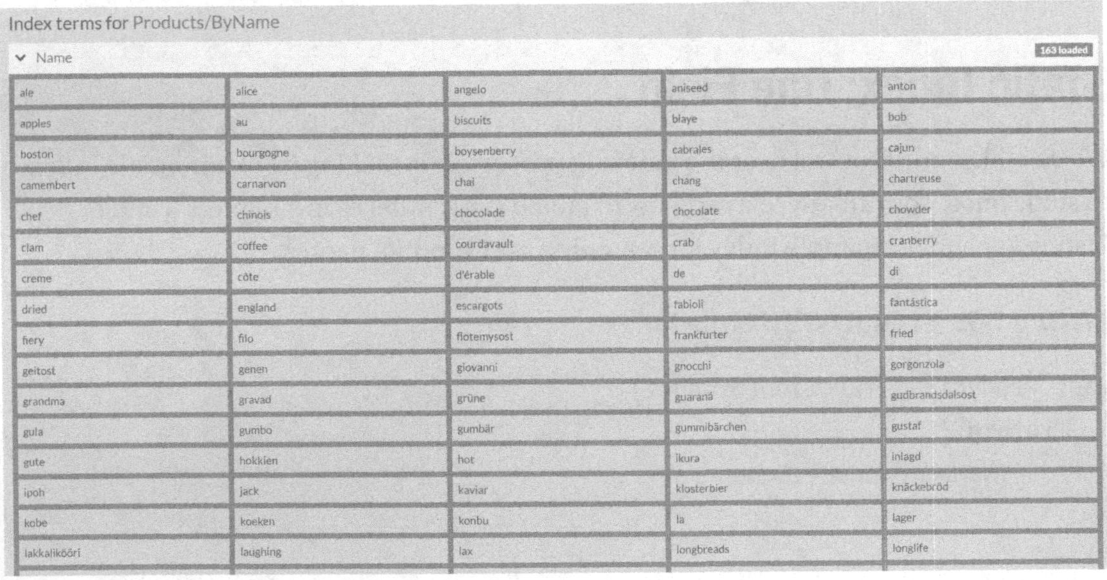

Figure 7-11. *Standard Analyzer Index Terms*

Looking at raw index entries for products, you can observe an array of tokens generated for every product by Standard Analyzer, as shown in Figure 7-12.

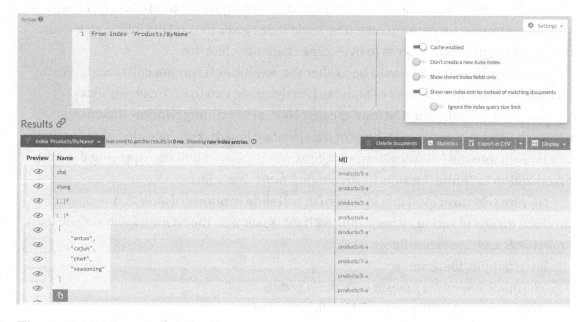

Figure 7-12. *Raw Index Entries*

We can now search for all lager beers:

```
from index 'Products/ByName'
where search(Name, "lager")
```

all product names starting with *cha*

```
from index 'Products/ByName'
where search(Name, "cha*")
```

or product names where any of the words end up with *ra*

```
from index 'Products/ByName'
where search(Name, "*ra")
```

Static Index: Different Analyzers

In one of the previous sections, we mentioned that using wildcard prefixes can have a significant impact on performance. The static index gives us total flexibility, so we can configure the indexing process to overcome challenges like this.

One possible solution would be to alter the way index terms are calculated. We can change tokenization - instead of Standard Analyzer, we can use *NGram Analyzer*.

But what does the word NGram means? NGram is a sliding window that moves across the text and produces tokens of the specified length. For example, word "brown" can be split into the following 3-grams: *[bro], [row], [own]*. Similarly, applying 2-grams tokenization to "jumps" results in stream *[ju], [um], [mp], [ps]*.

NGram tokenizer available in RavenDB will slide windows of sizes 2, 3, 4, 5, and 6 to produce tokens of various sizes. Along with this tokenizer, the NGram analyzer will use *StopWords* and *Lowercase* filters.

For example, for sentence

The quick brown fox jumped over the lazy dogs.

NGram analyzer will produce the following 3-grams:

```
[azy] [bro] [dog] [fox] [ick] [jum] [laz] [mpe] [ogs] [ove] [own] [ped]
[qui] [row] [uic] [ump] [ver]
```

The StopWords filter will eliminate two occurrences of "the" and the full stop.

You can now open the index *Products/ByName* defined in the previous section and change this index's analyzer. Scroll down to Fields and locate settings for the Name field. Click on *Standard Analyzer*, and you will be presented with a predefined list of analyzers, as shown in Figure 7-13.

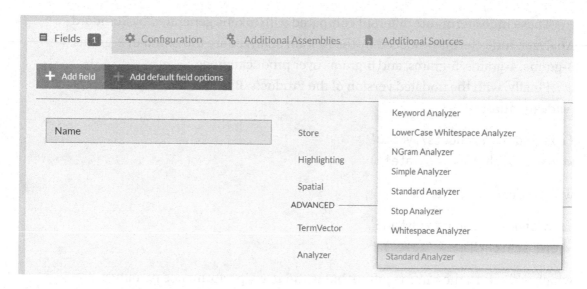

Figure 7-13. *Changing Index Analyzer*

After selecting *NGram Analyzer*, save redefined index.

Since you changed the definition of the index, RavenDB will build it from scratch by reading all documents from the Products collection, passing them through NGram Analyzer, and populating index terms. Figure 7-14 shows how index terms look now.

Index terms for Products/ByName				
∨ Name				500 loaded
'é	'ér	'éra	'érab	'érabl
aa	aan	aans	aanse	ab
abi	abio	abiol	abioll	abl
abie	abr	abra	abral	abrale
ac	acc	acca	ack	acl
acle	aclet	aclett	ad	ade
ads	af	ag	agd	age
ager	ai	aj	aju	ajun
ak	akk	akka	akkai	akkail
aku	al	ala	alac	alacc
alacca	alad	alade	ale	ales
ali	alic	alice	alik	alikö
aliköö	alk	alko	alkoi	alkoin
als	also	alsos	alsost	am
ame	amem	amemb	amembe	an
ana	anb	anbe	anber	anberr

Figure 7-14. *NGram Index Terms*

These index terms are different compared with tokens generated by Standard Analyzer. Index terms produced by the NGram analyzer are the union of 2-grams, 3-grams, 4-grams, 5-grams, and 6-grams over product names.

Finally, with the updated version of the Products/ByName index, we can replace the wildcard query:

```
from index 'Products/ByName'
where search(Name, '*late*')
```

with wildcard-free variant

```
from index 'Products/ByName'
where search(Name, 'late')
```

which will return the same result set but without any performance penalties.

Static Index: Multiple Fields

We defined and configured an index covering just one field in the previous two sections. This section will show how you can expand it to process multiple fields from documents belonging to one or more collections.

Indexing Property from Multiple Collections

We can expand *Products/ByName* into an index that will provide a way to search not only products by name but also Suppliers and Companies by name. This way, we will create one index that will cover the content of the documents from three collections.

Start by cloning the *Products/ByName* index – click the Clone button and change the name to *Search/ByName*.

Add the following two maps:

```
map("Companies", function(company) {
    return {
        Name: company.Name
    }
})
```

and

```
map("Suppliers", function(supplier) {
    return {
        Name: supplier.Name
    }
})
```

After you are done, the index definition will look as in Figure 7-15.

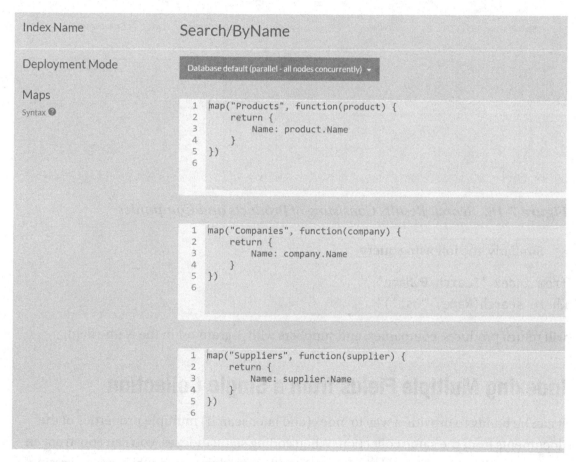

Index Name	Search/ByName
Deployment Mode	Database default (parallel - all nodes concurrently) ▾
| Maps<br>Syntax ❓ | ```
1  map("Products", function(product) {
2      return {
3          Name: product.Name
4      }
5  })
6
``` |
| | ```
1  map("Companies", function(company) {
2      return {
3          Name: company.Name
4      }
5  })
6
``` |
| | ```
1  map("Suppliers", function(supplier) {
2      return {
3          Name: supplier.Name
4      }
5  })
6
``` |

Figure 7-15. *Search/ByName Index*

Since we started by cloning the existing index *Products/ByName,* your newly created index supports full-text indexing on the *Name* field out of the box.

Now you can execute search queries that will span content from three collections.
```

Searching for

```
from index 'Search/ByName'
where search(Name, "cho")
```

will return products and companies with *cho* trigram in the Name, as shown in Figure 7-16.

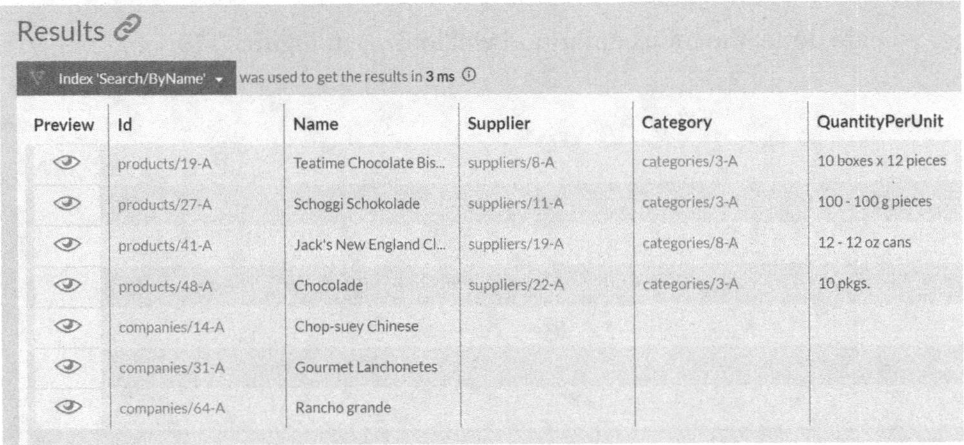

Results

Preview	Id	Name	Supplier	Category	QuantityPerUnit
👁	products/19-A	Teatime Chocolate Bis...	suppliers/8-A	categories/3-A	10 boxes x 12 pieces
👁	products/27-A	Schoggi Schokolade	suppliers/11-A	categories/3-A	100 - 100 g pieces
👁	products/41-A	Jack's New England Cl...	suppliers/19-A	categories/8-A	12 - 12 oz cans
👁	products/48-A	Chocolade	suppliers/22-A	categories/3-A	10 pkgs.
👁	companies/14-A	Chop-suey Chinese			
👁	companies/31-A	Gourmet Lanchonetes			
👁	companies/64-A	Rancho grande			

Index 'Search/ByName' was used to get the results in **3 ms**

Figure 7-16. *Search Results Consisting of Products and Companies*

Similarly, the following query

```
from index 'Search/ByName'
where search(Name, "ost")
```

will return products, companies, and suppliers with 3-gram *ost* in the Name field.

Indexing Multiple Fields from a Single Collection

It can be handy to provide a way to index (and later search) multiple properties of the documents from the same collection. When coding static indexes, you can construct an array that will hold several values. RavenDB will correctly process such arrays, creating multiple index terms per document.

Listing 7-8 shows an implementation of one such index. Do not forget to configure the *Query* field as a full-text search field.

Listing 7-8. Employees/ByFirstNameByLastName index

```
map("Employees", function(employee) {
    return {
        Query: [employee.FirstName, employee.LastName]
    }
})
```

Figure 7-17 shows that first and last names are extracted and inserted as index terms.

Index terms for Employees/ByFirstNameByLastName				
⌄ Query				18 loaded
andrew	anne	buchanan	caliahan	davolio
dodsworth	fuller	janet	king	laura
leverling	margaret	michael	nancy	peacock
robert	steven	suyama		

Figure 7-17. *Indexing Terms Consisting of First and Last Names of Employees*

With this index, you are now able to search by the first name:

```
from index 'Employees/ByFirstNameByLastName'
where search(Query, "Andrew")
```

or by the last name.

```
from index 'Employees/ByFirstNameByLastName'
where search(Query, "fuller")
```

Indexing Multiple Fields from Multiple Collections

The approach demonstrated in the previous section can be expanded further. Since you can load referenced documents during the indexing process, you can collect information from different collections to offer Omni search capabilities.

We could use arrays here to pack multiple properties together, but we will show an alternative approach, where we declare a JavaScript array and populate it from the code. Listing 7-9 shows the definition of the *Orders/Search* index. Create it in your database, and do not forget to mark the *Query* field as a full-text search field.

Listing 7-9. Orders/Search index

```
map("Orders", function(order) {
    var query = [];

    var company = load(order.Company, 'Companies');
    query.push(company.Name);

    var employee = load(order.Employee, 'Employees');
    query.push(employee.FirstName, employee.LastName);

    order.Lines.forEach (line => {
        var product = load(line.Product, 'Products');
        query.push(product.Name)

        var supplier = load(product.Supplier, 'Suppliers');
        query.push(supplier.Name);
    })

    return { Query: query }
})
```

Let's analyze this index.

The first line specifies the collection that will be processed – Orders. In the second line of the index definition, we are declaring an empty array:

```
var query = [];
```

which will be populated by the code. In the very end, our JavaScript code will return a field query with this very same array as content:

```
return { Query: query }
```

Furthermore, the referenced company is loaded for every order processed, and its name is added to the query array – same for referenced employees, considering they have first and last names. Finally, we iterate over order lines, fetch their product, and load a supplier for every product, adding their names to an array.

So, looking at the nesting of indexing levels, we have the following structure:

- Order
  - Company
  - Employee
  - OrderLine
    - Product
    - Supplier

We are descending three levels of references, loading referenced documents, and indexing their properties. Indexing terms will include names of companies, employees, products, and suppliers. With this index, you can search orders by various criteria.

For example, you can search for all orders created by Nancy:

```
from index 'Orders/Search'
where search(Query, "nancy")
```

All orders containing *tofu* can be fetched by executing the following query:

```
from index 'Orders/Search'
where search(Query, "tofu")
```

To see all orders related to a supplier *Lyngbysild*

```
from index 'Orders/Search'
where search(Query, "Lyngbysild")
```

Hence, you now have a single index that can serve queries by various criteria.

Summary

In this chapter, we covered the full-text search features of RavenDB. Besides introducing essential elements, we explained the inner workings of full-text search indexes. Finally, you learned about advanced indexing options and how to take more control over indexing with manually written static indexes.

Index

A

Abstraction, 34
Administration, 10
Advanced quering, 88, 89
    aggregation, 93–96
    declare functions, 92, 93
    include, 98, 99
    projecting with object literals, 90–92
    relationships, 96–98
Aggregates
    definition, 44
    denormalization, 44
    distributed systems, 47
    transaction boundaries, 47, 48
    unit of change, 44, 45
    unit of consistency, 45
Aggregation, 93–96, 147–149
Agile Manifesto, 8, 9
Artificial documents, 158, 159, 161
    create, 161–163
    indexing, 163, 164

B

Big data, 10
Bookstore, 34
boost() function, 178
Boosting, 178–181

C

Casing, 82, 83
Cloud computing, 8

Clustered index, 106
Collections, 27
Complex aggregation, 155
Computing, 1
Cost of storage, 8
Covering index, 107
Cross-collection query, 78, 79

D

Database management system (DBMS),
    1–3
Databases, 1
    DBMS, 1
    filtering, 103, 104
    NoSQL, 7
    paging, 102, 103
    RDBMS, 2
    relational model, 2
    unboubded queries, 101, 102
Data encapsulation, 38
Data integrity mechanisms, 63
Data model, 35
Distributed systems, 45, 46
Document-oriented models, 38
Document relationships
    many-to-many relationship, 67, 68
    one-to-many relationship
        best practice, 66
        checks, 66
        concurrency problems, 64
        exceptions, 66
        IDs of order, 64

© Dejan Miličić 2022
D. Miličić, *Introducing RavenDB*, https://doi.org/10.1007/978-1-4842-8919-8

Printed in the United States
by Baker & Taylor Publisher Services